Bible Repentance
Path to Love

Robert J. Wieland

Copyright © 2022 CFI Book Division

Cover and interior design by CFI Graphic Design

All rights reserved. No part of this book may be reproduced in any form or by any electronic or mechanical means including information storage and retrieval systems without permission from its publisher, CFI Book Division.

Original manuscript 1982

ISBN: 978-1-7344387-7-2

Published by CFI Book Division
P.O. Box 159, Gordonsville, Tennessee 38563

Contents

1. The Trial of God's Patience 1
2. Two Phases of Repentance 5
3. A Deeper Repentance That Pervades the "Body". 15
4. How Christ Repented of Sins He Never Committed . . . 21
5. How Jesus Called the Jews to National Repentance . . . 31
6. How the Jewish Nation Rejected Repentance 39
7. Christ's Call to the Church To Repent 47
8. How Can a Church of Millions of Members Repent? . . . 55
9. Corporate Repentance and Our Denominational History. . 63
10. Repentance: Path to Christlike Love 77

ADVENTIST ALL-AFRICA EDITORIAL CONSULTANT

The Seventh-day Adventist Church

June 8, 1982

Editorial Office:
Mitini Estate
P. O. Box 14756
NAIROBI, Kenya, East Africa

Dear Fellow Worker:

Enclosed please find a copy of a book manuscript, <u>Bible Repentance: Path to Love</u>.

This is the outgrowth of some 30 years of pondering our Lord's call to the last day church, "Be zealous therefore and repent." What does He mean when He says "repent"? Could it be that our failure to understand and respond to this call is the root source of our difficulties?

So far as I know, Seventh-day Adventists have never in all their history produced a book on the subject of repentance. It would seem that this is a field worthy of interest.

This manuscript was submitted to Pacific Press, Southern Publishing Association, and more recently the Review and Herald. In each instance the book committee rejected it.

Does that mean that this is the end of the world for this book on repentance? Can nothing more be done?

Perhaps there is fault in the manuscript that I as the author cannot see. I would be glad for someone more competent to write the book that needs to be written. But to date, I am not aware that anyone has undertaken this particular subject.

What is now my duty regarding this appeal to restudy our Lord's call to His last day church? Is there something further I can do?

Your counsel or criticisms would be helpful if you care to look this over and make comment. I would be grateful for your response.

Sincerely yours,

Robert J. Wieland
Adventist All Africa Editorial Consultant

RJW:gw

CHAPTER 1

THE TRIAL OF GOD'S PATIENCE

If God could be tempted to doubt, He would wonder (as we do) if it's just too good to be true: how can those thrilling prophecies in the Bible ever be fulfilled?

He has said in His word that the whole earth is to be "lightened with ... glory" (Revelation 18:1-4). That must include the entire Third World, Moslem lands, Communist nations, and the sensuous, materialistic West. This "light" is the message of "the everlasting gospel" which is to be given "mightily with a strong voice."

If the prophecy means what it says, it follows that everyone must hear the "voice" clearly. The results? They will be phenomenal, multitudes, far more than we think, will accept the "light." God's people will be astonished at the magnitude of the worldwide response (see Isaiah chapters 49-62).

The three angels of Revelation 14 and the fourth of chapter 18 are a symbol of the "remnant" church which is to be the agent in accomplishing this world-shaking mission. "The saints ... that keep the commandments of God, and the faith of Jesus" are to glorify Him amidst a world that disregards His holy law (Rev. 14:12). Naturally, the Lord wants very much to honor them before the world and the watching universe.

The Lord's Problem

But so long as His people continue to enjoy the material and social comforts of luxurious modern life, they may not feel the frustration that a century of delay in His schedule has brought to the heart of Christ. He is pained by this long drawn out wait. Can He be the unfeeling, impassive "thousand-years-as-a-day" Buddha that many have imagined Him to be? It is true that He is patient, and He wants all to be saved; but His patience can easily be misinterpreted as unconcern.

In reality, Revelation pictures our Lord as an eager Bridegroom who loves His church so much that he actually longs for the "marriage of the Lamb" to come soon (Rev. 19:7-9). He Himself deeply feels the on-going suffering of so many millions on this planet. An inspired glimpse of Him shows His true feelings about the long delay:

Leaving the first love is represented as a spiritual fall. Many have fallen thus. In every church in our land, there is needed confession, repentance, and reconversion. The disappointment of Christ is beyond description. (Ellen G. White, *Review and Herald*, Dec. 15, 1904).

We all recognize that we still await the coming of that mighty angel of Revelation 18 who is to join his voice in a loud cry with the third angel. The reason for the delay is simply that our Lord awaits our willingness to welcome this fourth angel, to sense our need for him. We may imagine we are doing fine without him; our Lord knows better. His people need a gift of heavenly efficiency if their message is to penetrate deeply into the heart-consciousness of the world.

Love is the Only Way

This grand finale of the work of the Holy Spirit will be a work of extraordinary beauty and simplicity:

> Those who wait for the Bridegroom's coming are to say to the people, "Behold your God." The last rays of merciful light, the last message of mercy to be given to the world, is a revelation of His character of love. The children of God are to manifest His glory. (*Christ's Object Lessons*, pp. 415, 416).

Once this Christlike love can permeate the church as a body, the message will indeed enlighten the earth in an incredibly short time. Human nature is the same the world over. Scratch the surface among all nations, races, or tribes, and one finds underneath the same human hunger for reality. The love of Christ manifested in human flesh is the universal language that will evoke a response everywhere.

How to achieve the active and powerful love as a body, so that the full resources and cohesion of the church can be perfectly used to demonstrate it to the world—this is our problem of surpassing importance. Can formal committee actions or high pressure promotion provide the needed motivation? No, These have all been tried repeatedly without real success. Truth must be the vehicle, because only truth can penetrate to the secret recesses of the human heart. The Lord has in reserve a means of motivation that will be truly effective. There will be no need to harangue God's people to respond, no need to provide artificial stimulation to induce them to put forth effort, any more than the apostles needed to in the beginning. Something happened at Pentecost that provided the early church with a truly phenomenal motivation.

That motivation was provided by an experience of full repentance, a doctrine that we shall see pervades both the Old and New Testaments. A hazy, indistinct concept of repentance can result only in a state of lukewarmness. Like medicine that must be taken in a quantity sufficient to provide a proper concentration in the blood stream, Bible repentance must be full and thorough or a truly Christlike love can never operate effectively in the church. This is the kind of repentance Christ demands of Laodicea.

This full spectrum of repentance is a truth that is included in "the everlasting gospel," but its clearest definition has been impossible until history reaches the time of the last of the "seven churches" of Revelation. This is because repentance can never be complete until the end of history. Repentance in the Greek is *metanoia*, from meta ("after") and nous ("mind").

That "end" could have come many decades ago if the "angel of the church of the Laodiceans" had been willing to receive the Lord's message when He says, "As many as I love, I rebuke and chasten: be zealous, therefore, and repent." (Rev. 3:19). We are still in this world of confusion and rebellion, battling still with evil spirits and wrestling with constantly worsening problems, for one simple reason: we have never truly done what our Lord has told us to do.

Repentance as a Motivational Force

Gadgets and inventions will never reveal God's love to the world. The only way possible to do it is to fill human hearts with it and let them personally be so full of it that it spills over naturally onto all whom we meet. "The children of God are to manifest His glory," that is, demonstrate His love. Waiting around for some new technological communication gimmick such as universal television "just around the corner" is vain. Our best method remains personal witnessing. Every new technological wonder (even satellites) can be expected to suffer exploitation by Satan. Christ must be manifested in the flesh; and that is why He has raised up a church world-wide.

But "personal witnessing" is idle talk unless we gain a heart experience parallel to that of Christ so that we have something urgent to witness about. And this becomes possible only by means of repentance.

Repentance is sorrow for sin and turning away from it. But if our view of sin is superficial, our repentance will likewise be superficial. Unless we truly appreciate the depth of our sin, only a veneer repentance becomes possible; and it is this that produces ever new generations of lukewarm church members. Sins that we are aware of can be the veneer, while there remains a deep subterranean stratum of sin which is unrealized, unconfessed, and therefore unforgiven. The repentance that our Lord calls for in these last days must be deep and thorough.

Repentance, rightly understood, will bring genuine unity in the church. "The mind of Christ" is a bridge between discordant elements within God's people. Our Saviour has often appealed to us, "Press together!" But this is impossible unless we press close to the cross in repentance. Without understanding our full guilt, repeated calls to the church to repent are virtually meaningless.

In the chapters to follow we shall search for an understanding of full and complete repentance, and see it illustrated in our Lord's own experience "in the flesh." We shall also see at least one historical precedent for a national repentance, a model which Christ set before the ancient Jewish nation for them to emulate. They decidedly and firmly rejected the "national" repentance He called for. We dare not repeat their history.

If our Lord is a personal Being who can feel a "disappointment ... beyond description," is it possible that our continued impenitence can at last change His frustration into anger?

If so, that would not be something pleasant to meet!

CHAPTER 2

TWO PHASES OF REPENTANCE

Jesus announced that His mission was to "call ... sinners to repentance" (Matthew 9:13). Such an experience is a personal change of mind, a turning around to go in the opposite direction. It includes deep heart sorrow for sin, a sense of shame and self-abhorrence for a life of rebellion against one's Creator and Redeemer. As such, it can be a cataclysmic upheaval of soul.

The way repentance works is clearly taught in the Bible. Jesus' call to repent is to all, for "all have sinned" (Romans 3:23). "The knowledge of sin" comes through "the law" (3:20). Thanks to the beneficent work of the Holy Spirit, this wholesome "knowledge" is imparted to "every man" as a "Light" that passes no one by (John 1:9).

This knowledge is imparted by a conviction that there is a standard of perfect righteousness in Christ. The sinner may as yet have never heard the name of Christ, but he knows deep in his heart that he has "sinned, and come short of the glory of God" (Romans 3:23).

The awareness of a perfect standard embodied in the law and in Christ may be ever so dim to consciousness, but Christ assured His disciples that as the result of His going to His Father "and ye see Me no more," the Holy Spirit would bring to the hearts of men a conviction of "sin, and of righteousness" (John 16: 8-10). This potential for the conviction of sin is as universal as is the capacity for pain built into every human body. It is a signal that something is wrong. Thus the Lord Himself who "so loved the world that He gave His only begotten Son" has prepared the way for the preaching of His gospel, which is complementary to this conviction of sin communicated by the Holy Spirit to "every man." When Jesus went forth after His baptism "preaching the gospel of the kingdom," His message was, "Repent ye, and believe the gospel" (Mark 1:14, 15).

Teaching legalism or an adulterated "gospel" short-circuits this work of the Holy Spirit in human hearts, and millions as a consequence are never able to receive the gift of repentance which alone can heal the "hurt" they feel. But Scripture foretells a time when the gospel will be restored and presented in its pristine purity and the earth will be "lightened" with its glory (Rev. 18:1-4). In millions of human lives it will be like restoring a broken electronic connection. The circuit will be complete—the Holy Spirit's conviction of sin will be complemented by the pure gospel, and the current of heaven's forgiveness will flow through the soul, working miracles of grace. This book is a search for that connection.

Man's Responses To God's Conviction Of Sin

A wound or injury to the body causes messages of pain to be relayed to the brain. Such pain can be alleviated by several methods of response. We can take a pain-killing drug and forget about the problem. This of course can lead to serious disease and death. But this is like what happens when the sinner rejects the "pain" of the Holy Spirit's merciful conviction of sin. An ability to feel pain in the body is a positive blessing, for it enables one to seek healing. The leper, whose sense of pain is anesthetized by his disease, actually suffers the loss of fingers and limbs because he does not feel destructive dangers to them. It is foolish and fatal to fight the Holy Spirit's conviction of sin. Repentance is the proper response of the human heart to the Holy Spirit's message of reproof or conviction of sin.

This true response to the conviction of sin is like seeking medicine or surgery for the healing of the body. The grateful sinner prays, "Thank You, Lord, for loving me so much as to convict me of my sin. I confess the full truth of the conviction, and acknowledge that sin has sentenced me justly to death. But I thank You that You have provided a Substitute who bears my penalty in my stead, and I am motivated by His love to separate from me the sin that has crucified Him." This was the miracle that occurred in David's heart when he prayed, "I will declare mine iniquity; I will be sorry for my sin" (Psalm 38:18).

Repentance And A New Life

Repentance is thus not only a sorrow for sin, but a genuine abhorrence of it. It is an actual turning away from sin, an awakened hatred of it. The law alone can never impart this phenomenal reaction; it must be combined with grace in order to be effective. "The law worketh wrath" and imparts a terror of judgement, but grace works the kind of repentance that makes "old things" to pass away; "behold, all things are become new" (2 Corinthians 5:17). Sin that was once loved is now hated; and God's righteousness is loved.

In this way, repentance is always associated with "remission of sins," that is, sending them away (Luke 24:47). In fact, the New Testament word for "forgiveness" implies a separation from sin, a deliverance from it. Repentance makes it actually impossible to continue in sin. The "love of Christ supplies the new motivation for a phenomenal change in the life (2 Corinthians 5:15, 15).

One finds a joyful sorrow in the experience:

The sadness that is used by God brings a change of heart that leads to salvation—and there is no regret in that! But sadness that is merely human causes death. See what God did with this sadness of yours: how earnest it has made you. ... Such indignation, such alarm, such feelings, such devotion. (2 Corinthians 7:10, 11, G.N.B.).

Peter is an example of such repentance. After basely denying his Lord with cursing and swearing, he "went out, and wept bitterly" (Mark 14:71; Luke 22:62). The weeping never ceased, for we are told that there was always afterward a tear glistening in his eyes as he thought of his sin in comparison with his Lord's grace. But they were happy tears, for the pain of contrition is always a rainbow glorified with the sunshine of divine forgiveness. Even medical scientists are beginning to recognize the wholesome healing therapy in such tears of contrition (see *Prevention*, August, 1980, pp. 126-130).

Far from being a negative experience of debilitating sorrow, such repentance is the foundation for all true joy. As every credit must have a corresponding debit to balance the books, so the smiles and happiness of life, in order to be meaningful, are founded on the tears of Another upon whom is "the chastisement of our peace" and with whose "stripes we are healed" (Isaiah 53:5). Repentance is not *our* tears and sorrow balancing the books of life; it is our appreciation of what it cost *Him* to do it, to bear our griefs and carry our sorrows (verse 4). It is in this sense that our repentance becomes a life-long experience:

> The nearer we come to Jesus, and the more clearly we discern the purity of His character, the more clearly shall we see the exceeding sinfulness of sin, and the less shall we feel like exalting ourselves. There will be a continual reaching out of the soul after God, a continual, earnest, heartbreaking confession of sin and humbling of the heart before Him. (*Acts of the Apostles*, p. 561).

At every advance step in Christian experience our repentance will deepen. It is to those whom the Lord has forgiven, to those whom He acknowledges as His people, that He says, "Then shall ye remember your own evil ways, and your doings that were not good, and shall loathe yourselves in your own sight. (Ezekiel 36:31). (*Christ's Object Lessons*, pp. 160, 161).

Such repentance is utterly beyond human capacity to invent or initiate. It must come from above. God has exalted Christ to be a "prince and a Saviour for to *give* repentance to Israel," said Peter (Acts 5:31). And to the Gentiles also He "granted repentance unto life" (Ch. 11:18). The capability for such a change of mind and heart is a priceless treasure from the Holy Spirit, something to covet above all else and to be profoundly thankful for. Even the will to repent is His gift, for without it we are all "dead in trespasses and sins" (Ephesians 2:1).

What Makes Repentance Possible?

The Bible links such repentance closely with faith. Paul testified "repentance toward God and faith toward our Lord Jesus Christ." (Acts 20:21). Repentance is therefore impossible without faith, and vice versa. It is not a cold calculation of options and their consequences, or a selfishly motivated choice to seek an eternal reward, or to flee the pains of hell. Repentance is a heart experience that results from appreciating the goodness of God. It cannot effectively be imposed by fear or terror, or even by hope of immortality. "The *goodness* of God leadeth thee to repentance" (Romans 2:4).

The ultimate source of this superb gift is the sacrifice of Christ on the cross. As faith is a heart-appreciation of the love of God revealed there, so repentance becomes the only appropriate decision the believing soul can make. It is the believing sinner's choice to follow where faith leads the way as illuminated by the cross. In fact, Peter's call to Israel to "repent, and be baptized every one of you" followed the most graphic sermon on the cross that has ever been preached (Acts 2:36-38). This phenomenal response at Pentecost became the direct fulfillment of Jesus' promise, "I, if I be lifted up from the earth, will draw all men unto Me" (John 12:32).

Genuine repentance with "works meet for repentance" is therefore as rare as that genuine preaching of the cross which constrains by the love of Christ (cf. Acts 26:20; 2 Corinthians 5:14). Its very essence is powerfully set forth in Isaac Watts' memorable words:

> When I survey the wondrous cross
>   On which the Prince of glory died,
> My richest gain I count but loss
>   And pour contempt on all my pride.

Thank God, this experience has not been unrealized. All through past ages, countless believing sinners have received this gift of personal repentance as bestowed by the Holy Spirit. Sleeping in the dust of the earth, they all await the "first resurrection." *Theirs has been one phase of repentance.*

The Key Factor in the First Resurrection

However, there must be a second coming of Christ, or this "first resurrection" can never take place. Further, without a preparation for His coming on the part of a unique people, He cannot come. Therefore, until He comes, the sleeping saints of all ages are doomed to remain prisoners in their dusty graves. Somehow, the vicious circle must be broken. Repentance is the vital factor. The key to unlock this log-jam of last day events is the heart-preparation of a people for translation without seeing death.

If this is true, it follows that there is a special sense in which Christ calls His people to repentance in these last days when He addresses "the angel" of the seventh church, the Laodiceans, "Be zealous therefore, and repent" (Revelation 3:14, 19).

His use of "therefore" is very significant. It refers to His enumeration of Laodicea's unusual problems of pride and her pathetic poverty. There are special reasons for this call to repent, special problems that will make Laodicea's ultimate response of repentance most unique.

What is Different About Laodicea's Repentance?

These problems do not necessarily mean that Laodicea is worse than the others of the seven churches; she seems as good as they. But such a standard is not sufficient for the immense eschatological opportunity of living in these last days, the time of the cleansing of the heavenly sanctuary. This never-before phase of our great High Priest's ministry calls for a never-before kind of response from His people. *This becomes another phase of repentance.*

In Christ's view, Laodicea's problem is that she is far behind the times in which she lives. Her spiritual condition has become an anachronism. She is "wretched, and miserable, and poor," while living in a time when she should enjoy unprecedented spiritual wealth. If one of us, accustomed to today's benefits of technology, were suddenly to return to living like a king or wealthy lord in the Dark Ages, he would be proper pitied as "wretched ... and poor" indeed. He would have no proper plumbing, no electricity, no furnace, no car, no phone, no TV, no medical care. Hardly any reader of this book would willingly return to such a primitive life, even in a medieval palace, with chamber-pots, spit-baths, and exposure to the Black Plague. Jesus says that Laodicea is "wretched" because the spiritual wealth of past ages becomes "miserable" in a time when spiritual progress is possible beyond any previous age. While Christ is performing His "final atonement" in the second apartment of the heavenly sanctuary, for us to continue living as though He were still in the first apartment—this is poverty indeed. The setting of the Laodicean message is the Day of Atonement.

Another problem is that the remnant church is also "blind and naked." Although she is living in the time of judgment, she is shamefully unprepared, pitifully ignorant of how she appears before the watching eyes of the world and the universe. The pathos of her true state is beyond words. Is it not the ultimate shame to be naked, and yet be unaware of it? "Thou knowest not," says the True Witness. And even worse than being naked and not knowing it, to imagine that one is "rich and increased with goods"—this borders on actual lunacy. The gap between Laodicea's unique opportunities just before the coming of Christ and her true state has widened so much that her pathetic condition has become the most difficult problem the Lord has ever had to deal with. Laodicea is the laughing stock of hell.

If her condition is unique, surely the repentance Christ calls for from her must also be unique. *What kind of repentance could possibly match Laodicea's need?*

At the risk of over-simplifying the answer, we could say that Laodicea's repentance today must be appropriate to the ministry of Christ in cleansing the heavenly sanctuary. It must be the kind of repentance that fits the Day of Atonement, because the message to Laodicea is parallel to this cleansing of the sanctuary. To say this in words is easy, and is true enough; how to discover what this means in practical, understandable terms—this is our task.

Repentance and the Cleansing of the Sanctuary

One helpful clue is provided by the Bible doctrine of the "blotting out of sins" which takes place in "the times of refreshing," that is, the cleansing of the sanctuary (see Acts 3:19). Seventh-day Adventists understand the "daily" ministry in the sanctuary to include the forgiveness of sins; but the "yearly" includes the blotting out of sins. This work, which we understand began in 1844, is something that occurs only at the end of time, the conclusion of the 2300 years (see *The Great Controversy*, pp. 421, 422, 483).

But just as no sin can be *forgiven* without appropriate repentance, likewise no sins can be *blotted out* without appropriate repentance. It is obvious that in these last days there is something Laodicea "knows not," some deeper level of guilt and sin which has never been discerned nor truly repented of. And Christ calls Laodicea to such a repentance.

It will not suffice for one to say, "Let the heavenly computers do the work—my sins will be blotted out when the time comes without my knowing about it." This may be partly true; but there is no such thing as automatic, computerized blotting out of sins that takes place without our participation and cooperation. It is we who are to repent individually, not the heavenly computers. No sin can be forgiven or blotted out unless we come to see it, confess it, and turn from it. Our deeper level of sin and guilt must be realized if our Saviour's complete ministry for us is to be effected. Nothing short of this can be true repentance in such a time as this.

Hence there lies before Laodicea an experience of repentance that is unique in world history. The Lord calls for it *now*. All things are being held up for lack of it. Our plane, freighted with the precious cargo of the Loud Cry message to enlighten the earth, has been circling in a holding pattern far too long. There is no time now for more delay, not even to wait until after the "shaking," for then it may be too late.

Ellen G. White had a profound understanding of human nature. She recognized the existence of a deeper level of sinful guilt beneath the surface of our understanding, and how, if we let Him, our great High Priest will bring this to our understanding so that repentance can be complete. The principle is clear:

> The work of restoration can never be thorough unless the *roots* of evil are reached. Again and again the shoots have been clipped, while the root of bitterness has been left to spring up and defile many; but *the very depth of the hidden evil* must be reached, the moral senses must be judged, and judged again, in the light of the divine presence. (*SDA Bible Commentary*, Vol. 5, p. 1152).

> The Laodicean message must be proclaimed with power; for now it is especially applicable. ... Not to see our own deformity is not to see the beauty of Christ's character. When we are *fully awake to our own sinfulness*, we shall appreciate Christ. ... Not to see the marked contrast between Christ and ourselves is not to know ourselves. He who does not abhor himself cannot understand the meaning of redemption. ... There are many who do not see themselves in the light of the law of God. They do not loathe selfishness; therefore they are selfish. (*Review and Herald*, Sept. 25, 1900).

> The message to the Laodicean church reveals our condition as a people. ... Ministers and church-members are in danger of allowing self to take the throne. ... If they would *see* their defective, distorted characters as they are accurately reflected in the mirror of God's word, they would be so alarmed that they would fall upon their faces before God in contrition of soul, and tear away the rags of their self-righteousness. (*Ibid.*, Dec. 15, 1904).

> The Holy Spirit will reveal faults and defects of character that ought to have been discerned and corrected. ... The time is near when the *inner life* will be fully revealed. All will behold, as if reflected in a mirror, the working of the *hidden springs of motive*. The Lord would have you now examine your own life, and see how stands your record with Him. (*Ibid.*, Nov. 10, 1896).

> If we have defects of character of which we are not aware, He [the Lord] gives us discipline that will bring those defects to our knowledge, that we may overcome them. ... Your circumstances have served to bring new defects in your character to your notice; but *nothing is revealed but that which was in you*. (*Ibid.*, Aug. 6, 1889; all emphasis in above quotations is supplied).

It is only to be expected that the enemy of Christ will put forth the most diabolic and persistent efforts to prevent or delay this full repentance which He calls for. Satan is delighted to see God's people continue proudly in their self-satisfied and lukewarm state, decade after decade. He sneers contemptuously at their spiritual naivete, while they are unknowing of their shame. His purpose is to expose them to the scorn of the world and keep them the objects of Heaven's shame.

The Greatest Sin of All the Ages

Israel's ruin came because they refused in the days of their Messiah to accept His message concerning a deeper level of guilt than they had realized. They were not by nature more evil than any other generation; it was simply theirs to act out to the full the same sinfulness that all the fallen sons and daughters of Adam have by nature. To them the divine Son of God came on a mission of mercy. As our natural "carnal mind is enmity against God" (Romans 8:7), they simply demonstrate this fact visibly, once for all, in the murder of their divine Visitor. All of us must know that we are by nature no better than they. Those who crucified the Saviour are only holding up a mirror wherein we can see ourselves.

Horatius Bonar learned this in a dream. One night he seemed to be witnessing the crucifixion of Christ. In a frenzy of agony, such as we experience in vivid dreams, he tried to remonstrate with the cruel soldiers who were driving spikes through Christ's hands and feet. He laid his hand on the shoulder of one of them to beg him to stop. When the murderer turned to look at him, Bonar recognized his own face.

The repentance which Christ calls for from Laodicea is that which will go down to the deepest roots of this natural "enmity against God." What is this deeper phase of repentance? *It is repenting of sins that we may not have personally committed, but which we would have committed if we had the opportunity.* This is appropriate because the books of heaven already record those sins written against our names:

> God's law reaches the feelings and motives, as well as the outward acts. It reveals the secrets of the heart, flashing light upon things before buried in darkness. God knows every thought, every purpose, every plan, every motive. The books of heaven record the sins that would have been committed had there been opportunity. (*SDA Bible Commentary*, Vol. 5, p. 1085)

Everyone of us can ask himself the profound question, what sins would I have committed "had there been opportunity"? Linger for a moment on that word, "opportunity." It has come to others in the form of alluring, overmastering temptations. The tempter sees to it that "opportunity" is available through fiendishly clever circumstances and temptations.

None of us can endure the full consciousness of what we would do if subjected to sufficient pressure, terrorism for example. But our potential sin is recorded in "the books of heaven." Only the full work of the Holy Spirit can bring to us this deeper conviction of sin; but in these last days when sins must be "blotted out" as well as pardoned, this is His blessed work. No buried seed of sin can be translated into God's eternal kingdom.

Therefore, the kind of repentance Christ calls for from His people in these last days is repenting as though what is apparently the sin of others were really our own (which in fact it is). Whatever sins other people are guilty of, they obviously had the "opportunity" of committing them; somehow the temptations were real to them and overmastering. The deeper insight the Holy Spirit brings us in these last days is that we are by nature no better than other sinners are. When Scripture says that "all have sinned," it means, as the New English Bible translates it, "all alike have sinned" (Romans 3:23).

The root of all sin, its common denominator, is of course the crucifixion of Christ, enmity against God. A confession of sin that only scratches the surface can bring only a veneer forgiveness. A terrible record remains upon the books of heaven, even though we are not aware of it—"thou knowest not."

What kind of repentance is Christ calling for in these last days? How deep and thorough must it be? What are the practical aspects of this tremendous disclosure of our true guilt?

Our search must continue.

CHAPTER 3

A DEEPER REPENTANCE THAT PERVADES THE "BODY"

Most of us are deeply thankful for the church as a "body" of believers in Christ. Around the world there are some solitary, isolated believers deprived of the warm fellowship most of us enjoy. It's no fun being alone, especially with an unpopular faith. We like being a part of "the body."

A person is more than a scattered assortment of limbs, organs, or cells. All these organs of a "body" thrive on a vital relationship together. None could survive alone. Such is the church. Christ is "the Head," and we are all individually "members of His body."

In fact, no individual believer in Christ could possibly reveal all the infinite facets of the Saviour's character, any more than a single part of one's body could express or fulfill all of the thoughts or intents of the head. The feet, for example, can do some things the hands can't do and vice versa. Each of us is needed in order to reflect to the world and the universe all those aspects of the loveliness of Christ's character. If we don't realize this, sinful pride can force us to exhibit to the world a deformed representation of the body of Christ.

The apostle Paul grasped the idea of this vital member-to-member-to-Christ relationship. Truly inspired by the Holy Spirit, his illustration is brilliant.

Everyone can understand it, even children. It is almost as if the human body had been created just to provide this perfect symbol of the relationship the church bears to the world and to Christ.

> Christ is like a single body with its many limbs and organs, which, many as they are, together make up one body. ... A body is not a single organ, but many. ... God appointed each limb and organ to its own place in the body, as He chose. If the whole were one single organ, there would not be a body at all; in fact, however, there are many different organs, but one body. ... God has combined the various parts of the body, giving special honour to the humbler parts, so that there might be no sense of division in the body, but that all its organs might feel the same concern for one another. If one organ suffers, they all suffer together. ... Now you are Christ's

body, and each of you is a limb or organ of it. (1 Corinthians 12:12-27, NEB).

The Meaning of the Word "Corporate"

The word "body" is a noun, and the word "bodily" is an adverb; but there is no English adjective that can describe the nature of this relationship within the "body," except the word "corporate" from the Latin word for body. Webster's Seventh New Collegiate Dictionary defines it as "of or relating to a whole composed of individuals." Corporate guilt is becoming a well-known theological term. For example, Senator Mark Hatfield presented a resolution to Congress in January, 1974, saying, "I believe that only a national confession of corporate guilt can save us." In his Second Inaugural Address Abraham Lincoln recognized the corporate guilt of the entire nation for the sin of slavery.*

If you stub your toe badly, you will realize this corporate relationship of the limbs and organs of your body. You stop while your whole body cooperates in an effort to rub that sore toe and lessen the pain. You may even hurt all through your body. All your various organs and limbs feel a corporate concern for that wounded toe, as if each feels the pain.

Any illness or amputation in the body becomes a "schism" to be avoided at almost any cost. Likewise, any measure of disunity or misunderstanding, or lack of compassion in the church, is foreign to Christ and His body, as alien as disease or an accident is to our human body. Sin is such an accident to the "body of Christ," and guilt is its disease.

The wounded toe may be the individual that suffers, but the whole body suffers with it. The other members may be conceived as feeling responsible for the wound, the leg saying, "Had I been more careful, the toe would not have been stubbed," or the eye saying, "If I had been more watchful, it wouldn't have happened." "If one organ suffers, they all suffer together." 1 Corinthians 12:26, NEB. The idea of corporate sin and guilt is implicit in Paul's inspired illustration.

---

* See *Christianity Today,* February 1, 1974 and March 12, 1971, article by Vance Havner; and Abraham Lincoln's proclamation for a "National Day for Humiliation, Fasting, and Prayer" of April 30, 1863.

Often we humans suffer from mysterious diseases that lay us low, without our even knowing what organ is ill, or what causes the sickness. Could our Laodicean disease of lukewarmness be something similar? Could there be in our hearts today a depth of guilt that we do not realize or understand?

Are Some Lions "Good" and Some "Bad"?

Some lions in Africa become man-eaters; but the vast majority never get a taste of human beings. Does this mean that most lions are "good" and only a few are "bad"? Is there a difference in lions so far as "character" is concerned?

The fact is that all lions are alike, and given the proper circumstances, any lion will be a man-eater. When he becomes weak or old, separated from the pride which would normally supply him with food, he readily turns to man-eating. We noticed in our last chapter Ellen White's disturbing statement, "The books of heaven record the sins that would have been committed had there been opportunity." A man-eating lion is simply acting out his basic nature and we can be thankful that most of them don't get the "opportunity" to demonstrate it fully!

What is our basic nature as sinners? The answer is obvious, but very unpalatable to recognize: we are at enmity with God by nature, and await only the proper circumstances to demonstrate it by crucifying the Son of God. This is the ultimate measure of our corporate guilt.

A familiar disease may help to illustrate our relationship as a body. In malarial areas, people are often bitten by the anopheles mosquito, and infected with malarial parasites. Some ten days after the bite, the parasites in the blood stream produce malarial fever. Not only is the one "member" affected which actually received the mosquito bite, such as the finger, but the whole body partakes of the common fever. The blood stream has carried the parasites all over the body. Let us call this a "corporate" disease, for that is what it is.

We then receive an injection of an anti-malarial drug in one "member," perhaps the arm or the hip. The one "member" receiving the injection is not the only one to benefit. The parasite-destroying medicine begins to course throughout the blood stream. Soon the entire body is healed of the disease, and the fever disappears over all the body, not just in the one "member." The injection has provided a "corporate" healing.

In order to understand what full repentance is, we need to understand our corporate relationship to the entire human race "in Adam." The entire body feels the fever of the malarial infection. So did Christ feel the weight of the sins of the world. This we must appreciate, if we are to appreciate His healing. As long as we feel that we have escaped infection by the common parasite of sin "in Adam," as long as we feel superior to other "sinners" simply because the infection happened not to occur in our particular "member," we will be unable to share in the corporate healing provided by Christ. This means that we are powerless to help another person find deliverance from his sin if we in superiority refuse to feel the weight of his guilt. In order to feel this weight we do not need to repeat his actual sinful deed. By sensing the reality or corporate guilt and repentance, we put ourselves in his place. As we shall see in the next chapter, Christ has shown us the way.

A Portrait of Christ and of His Body

Marvelous will be the results when God's people as a church learn to love sinners as Christ loves them. The only way He has to show that love to them is through His church on earth. Therefore "God hath set ... in the church" the various gifts of His Spirit so that the church may become His efficient "body" for expressing Himself to the world in the same way that a healthy person expresses through the "members" of his physical body the thoughts and intent of his mind. These "gifts" lead up to the supreme gift of love, which Paul says is "a more excellent way."

1 Corinthians 12 discusses the corporate relationship of the "many members" with one another and with Christ in the church, "the body." The "more excellent way" of love is revealed in chapter 13 as the normal function of the "body," its corporate effectiveness in service. The two chapters must not be separated. Many have seen in chapter 13 a "portrait" of Christ. But in its full context the portrait really is of the church. Paul added the 13th to the 12th chapter in order to demonstrate how the union of the "many members" with Christ as "the Head" works out in practical life. The "many members" in "one body" in Christ become the actual body of Christ on earth for the great purpose of expressing His

love to a world that is dark with misapprehension of God. And every member is needed for this glorious work to be effective!

Here in 1 Corinthians 13 is a picture of the church in the time of the final outpouring of the Holy Spirit. Every individual church becomes in its respective community what Christ would be to that community if He were living there in the flesh. Thus His love is communicated effectively to the world, and the lines will be clearly drawn. All men will decide for or against this final revelation. And thus the Lord's prophecy will be completely fulfilled: "This gospel of the kingdom shall be preached in all the world for a witness to all nations; and then shall the end come." Matthew 24:14.

When the members of the body perform naturally the intents and feelings of the head, there is perfect bliss. Imagine if you will the most delightful enjoyments that the body experiences when there is no conflict between the intent of the mind and the pleasures of the physical senses. Each organ of the body cooperates in perfect unity; the combination of physical and mental joy is indescribable. "So also is Christ" (1 Corinthians 12:12). The perfect joy the human personality experiences is a symbol of the perfect joy the church experiences. "There should be no schism [paralysis] in the body; ... the members should have the same care one for another" (verses 25, 26). There is no breakdown of the vital system of nerve pathways conveying communication between the "Head" and the "body."

Repentance is this nerve pathway that will communicate this effective love to every member of Christ's body.

CHAPTER 4

HOW CHRIST REPENTED OF SINS HE NEVER COMMITTED

Both the Bible and the Spirit of Prophecy make it clear that Jesus Christ experienced repentance. This does not mean that He experienced sin, for never in thought, word, or deed did He yield to temptation. Peter says, "Who did no sin, neither was guile found in His mouth." 1 Peter 2:22. When John the Baptist baptized Jesus, it was because Jesus asked for it, and insisted upon it. If "John verily baptized with the baptism of repentance" (Acts 19:4), he must have baptized Jesus with the only baptism he was capable of administering—a baptism signifying on the part of the sinless Candidate an experience of repentance.

But how could Christ experience repentance if He had never sinned? This is a most important question, for multitudes of saints are ready to ask, "How can *I* repent of sins I have never committed?" We have assumed that only evil people need to repent, or can repent. It is shocking to think that *good* people can repent, and incomprehensible how a *perfect* Person could repent.

If Christ was "baptized with the baptism of repentance," it is clear that He did experience it. But the only kind of repentance a sinless person could experience is corporate repentance. Thus, Jesus' repentance is a model and example of what we ourselves should experience.

Jesus' Baptism Unto Repentance

Jesus was genuinely sincere when He asked John to baptize Him. When He answered John's objections at the Jordan, "Thus it becometh us to fulfill all righteousness" (Matthew 3:15), it is unthinkable that He was suggesting that He and John should together act out a play. Play-acting could never "fulfill all righteousness." The essence of righteousness is sincerity and genuineness. Our divine Example could never condone the performance of such a rite without the appropriate experience of heart. For Christ to subject Himself to baptism without an experience appropriate to the deed would have been to give an example of hypocrisy. Shallow formalism or hypocrisy is the last thing Jesus wants from anyone!

It is easy for us to misunderstand Jesus' baptism as merely a "deposit" of merit to be drawn on in a legalistic substitutionary way in certain emergencies when people cannot be baptized for physical reasons, such as the predicament of the thief on the cross. One must be baptized before he can enter Paradise; the poor thief is nailed to a cross and therefore cannot be immersed; Jesus' baptism becomes to him like a credit in the "bank", and the appropriate "deposit" is made to the account of the poor thief. We have supposed that the reason Jesus was baptized was to provide this "credit" balance of merit. The poor thief's "account" is duly credited, and he is promised a place in Paradise.

Whatever elements of truth may lurk in this legalistic concept, the idea leaves us "cold." Most Christians have had the physical opportunity to be immersed in baptism, and have complied. What does Jesus' baptism mean to them? Merely a physical demonstration of the *method* of baptism? Merely that we have seen the "Teacher" act out the physical deed He asks us to do? Once the truth of corporate repentance is recognized, Jesus' baptism takes on a meaningful significance. Hearts are touched and won by saving truth.

How Close Jesus Came to Us

Jesus indeed asked for baptism because He genuinely and sincerely identified Himself with sinners. He felt how the guilty sinner feels. He put Himself in our place. He put His arms around us and knelt down beside us on the banks of the Jordan, taking our sins upon Himself. His submission to baptism indicates that "the Lord ... laid on Him the iniquity of us all" then and there. His baptism becomes an "injection" of healing repentance for sin into the "body" of the church. Peter says that His identity with our sins was deep, not superficial, for "His own self bare our sins *in His own body*." Peter's choice of words is significant. Christ did not bear our sins as a man carries a bag on his back. In His own "flesh," in His nervous system, He bore the crushing weight of our guilt. So close did He come to us that He felt our sins were His own.

This perfect identity with us began long before Calvary. Ellen G. White offers this perceptive comment on the reality of Christ experiencing a deep heart repentance in our behalf:

> After Christ had taken the necessary steps in repentance, conversion, and faith in behalf of the human race, He went to John to be baptized of him in Jordan. (1901 *General Conference Bulletin*, p. 36.)

John had heard of the sinless character and spotless purity of Christ. ... John had also seen that He should be the example for every repenting sinner John could not understand why the only sinless one upon the earth should ask for an ordinance implying guilt, virtually confessing, by the symbol of baptism, pollution to be washed away. ... , Christ came not confessing His own sins; but guilt was imputed to him as sinner's substitute. He came not to repent on His own account; but in behalf of the sinner. ... As their substitute, He takes upon Him their sins, numbering Himself with the transgressors, taking the steps the sinner is required to take; and doing the work the sinner must do. (*Review and Herald*, January 21, 1873.)

Let us take a second look at the important points in these statements:

(a) Though Christ was utterly sinless, He did in His own soul experience repentance.

(b) His baptism indicated that He felt in His own sinless heart the burden of guilt that oppresses the heart of the sinner. In other words, He knows exactly how the sinner feels, including "every repenting sinner." In our self-righteousness we cannot feel such sympathy with "every repenting sinner" because only a Perfect Man can experience a perfect and complete repentance such as that.

(c) Not in pantomime, but in verity, Jesus took "the steps the sinner is required to take," and did "the work the sinner must do." This implies a reality of identity with us. We cannot in truth "behold the Lamb of God which taketh away the sin of the world" without appreciating how close our Lord has come to us in His human experience. This is why it is so important to "behold" Jesus, to "see" Him. Lukewarm impenitence is due either to not seeing Him clearly revealed, or to rejecting Him. Let us take a closer look at "the Lamb of God, which taketh away the sin of the world," and understand what our sin is that needs to be "taken away," so that it indeed can be taken away.

Why did Jesus, in His ministry, have such phenomenal power to win the hearts of sinners? Because in this pre-baptism experience of "repentance, conversion, and faith in behalf of the human race," Jesus learned to know what was "in man," for "He needed not that any should testify of man" (John 2:25). Only through such an experience could He learn to speak as "never man spake" (John 7:46). Only thus could He break the spell of the world's enchantment as He would say to whom He would,

"Follow me," passing by no human being as worthless, inspiring with hope the "roughest and most unpromising." "To such a one, discouraged, sick, tempted, fallen, Jesus would speak words of tenderest pity, words that were needed and could be understood." (*Ministry of Healing*, p. 26.) It may be getting ahead of ourselves to take notice of this point right now, but it begins to be apparent that we ourselves will be able to achieve such empathy with sinners only when we have experienced the kind of repentance that Christ experienced in our behalf.

The "How" of Jesus' Power to Reach Hearts

Jesus' perfect compassion for every human soul is, as Son of God, a direct result of His perfect repentance in behalf of every human soul. He becomes the "second Adam," partaking of the "body," becoming one with us, accepting us as His "brethren" without shame, "in all things ... made like unto His brethren."

We freely recognize our desperate need of this genuine, deep, unfailing Christ-like love for sinners. We can preach about it for a thousand years, but we will never get it except through faith in the Lord Jesus Christ. And such faith is a heartfelt appreciation of His character. A union with Christ that goes beyond mere theory is our desperate need.

But trying to come close to Christ without coming close to sinners is impossible, for through union with Christ by faith we become part of the corporate body of humanity in Him. "As in Adam all die, even so in Christ shall all be made alive" (1 Corinthians 15:22). Although He did not personally participate in our sin, He became a part of us, bearing the guilt of the human race. It is the purest selfishness to want to appropriate Christ, yet refuse to receive His love for sinners!

In fact, we have infinitely more reason to feel a kinship with sinners than did our sinless Lord, for we ourselves *are* sinners; but we find that our natural human pride too easily holds us back from the warm empathy that Christ felt for them. How to learn to experience this kinship is our need.

There is no better way to begin than by learning to recognize the truth of our corporate involvement in the sin of the whole world. Although we were not physically present at the events of Calvary two thousand years ago, "in Adam" the whole human race was there. As surely as we are by nature "in Adam," so surely are we in Adam's sin.

How can this be so?

Let any of us be left without redemption to develop to the full the evil latent in his own soul, let him be left to be tempted to the full as others have been tempted, and he will duplicate the sin of others if given enough time and opportunity. None of us dares to say, "I could never do that!"

If Abraham's great-grandson "yet in the loins" of Abraham "when Melchisedeck met him" paid tithes "in Abraham," it is easy to see how every one of us partakes together of the corporate body of humanity. If Levi paid tithes "in Abraham," so do we, for we are Abraham's spiritual descendants as much as Levi was. (see Hebrews 7:9, 10).

In the same way, we partake of the corporate sin of humanity in the crucifixion of Christ at Calvary. The sin of sins that underlies all sin, and of which we are all alike guilty in a corporate sense, is the murder of the Son of God.

Repentance Precedes Forgiveness

Many cannot sense how they are in any way responsible for a sin that was committed by other people in another land in another age, nearly two thousand years before they were born. But here is the very heart of the gospel itself: the "good news" tells us that God forgives us that sin. *But how can we receive forgiveness for a sin we don't feel guilty of committing?* The apostle John tells us that it is only when we confess a sin that we can experience Christ's "faithful" forgiving and cleansing from it (1 John 1:9).

But to confess a sin without sensing its reality is mere lip-service, perilously close to hypocrisy. Skin-deep confession, surface repentance, bring skin-deep love, surface devotion.

Jesus teaches that we must feel we have been "forgiven much" before we can possibly learn to "love much." (see Luke 7:14).

Note how an inspired comment clearly involves us all in the guilt of crucifying Christ:

> That prayer of Christ for His enemies embraced the world. It took in every sinner that had lived or should live, from the beginning of the world to the end of time. Upon all rests the guilt of crucifying the Son of God. (*Desire of Ages*, p. 745.)

The world was stirred by the enmity of Satan, and when asked to choose between the Son of God and the criminal Barabbas, they chose a robber rather than Jesus. ... Let us all remember that we are still in a world where Jesus, the Son of God, was rejected and crucified, where the guilt of despising Christ and preferring a robber rather than the spotless Lamb of God still rests. Unless we individually repent toward our Lord Jesus Christ, whom the world has rejected, we shall lie under the full condemnation that the action of choosing Barabbas instead of Christ merited. The whole world stands charged today with the deliberate rejection and murder of the Son of God. The word bears record that Jews and Gentiles, kings, governors, ministers, priests, and people—all classes and sects who reveal the same spirit of envy, hatred, prejudice, and unbelief, manifested by those who put to death the Son of God—would act the same part, were the opportunity granted, as did the Jews and people of the time of Christ. They would be partakers of the same spirit that demanded the death of the Son of God. (*Testimonies to Ministers*, p. 38.)

These astounding statements deserve a second look:

(a) The guilt of crucifying Christ "still rests" upon the world, even upon "every sinner." Even "ministers" and church members partake of this sin. Apart from the grace of God manifested through repentance, we each share the guilt.

(b) Without this grace, "every sinner" would repeat the sin of Christ's murderers if given enough time and opportunity.

The sin of Calvary is seen to be an out-cropping of a sub-stratum of sin which men are not aware of except by enlightenment of the Holy Spirit. At Calvary, every man's sin is fully unmasked. We can't "see" it until we "see" Calvary.

In a very real sense we were each one at Calvary, not through pre-existence or pre-incarnation, but in the sense of corporate identity "in Adam." If it is true that "upon all rests the guilt of crucifying the Son of God," Adam likewise partakes of that guilt equally with us today. His sin in the Garden of Eden was to Calvary what the acorn is to the oak.

(e) The "righteous" in their own eyes, including "ministers" and "priests" of "all ... sects," are potentially capable of revealing "the same spirit" as was manifested by those who actually crucified Christ. This statement includes Seventh-day Adventists.

The Acorn Produces the Oak

Every one of us is born with the "carnal mind" which is "enmity against God," and the little acorn of our "carnal mind" needs only enough time to grow into the full oak of the sin of Calvary. But he who has "the mind of Christ" will have the repentance of Christ. Therefore, the closer he comes to Christ, the more he will identify himself with every sinner on earth.

In order for Christ's righteousness to cover our sin, the principle of identity must work both ways; whereas He identifies Himself with every sinner on earth, we must do the same. Until we do, all our claims to be "covered" with the righteousness of Christ are empty and futile. If we would accept the gracious provision that "in Christ shall all be made alive" we must recognize the equal truth that "in Adam all die."

This simple truth found in the New Testament shatters self-esteem and complacency. Once let Paul's truth of corporate identity be recognized, we begin to appreciate something of the guilt of the sins of the world and our smug superiority is melted down to deep contrition and love for "every repenting sinner" on the face of the earth. Immediately we feel in our hearts that we are "debtor both to the Greeks, and to the barbarians." The miracle of miracles takes place in our proud lukewarm hearts: *we begin to love sinners exactly like Christ loves them.*

To make this very practical, how did Christ love sinners? If He were to come into our churches today, we might be scandalized.

He "recognized no distinction of nationality, or rank or creed ..., His gift of mercy and love ... as unconfined as the air, the light, or the showers of rain that refresh the earth." He "came to break down every wall or partition." In Christ's example "there is no caste, a religion by which Jew and Gentile, free and bond, are linked in a common brotherhood, equal before God. No question of policy influenced His movements. He made no difference between neighbors and strangers, friends and enemies. ... He passed by no human being as worthless, but sought to apply the healing remedy to every soul. ... Every neglect or insult shown by men to their fellow men, only made Him more conscious of their need of His divine-human sympathy. He sought to inspire with hope the roughest and most unpromising." (*Ministry of Healing*, pp. 25, 26.)

This is exactly the kind of practical love that corporate repentance produces in any human heart that will receive the gift. The "injection" of Christ's corporate repentance produces a love that permeates His body, the church. No longer are we hopeless to "reach" the sinner in modern times whose particular evil deeds we do not understand and pride ourselves on not having committed. Corporate repentance enables us to bridge the gap that insulates us from needy souls whom Christ loves, but for whom He can exercise no healing ministry because we as His instruments are "frozen" in our unfeeling impenitence.

Like Christ "who did no sin" but knew repentance, so we can feel a genuine compassion in behalf of others whose sins we may not personally have committed, either for lack of opportunity or for lack of temptation of equal intensity. Forthwith we begin helping them. Our work for them "comes alive," and we find our efforts become effective. Love is freed from the chains of our impenitence and immediately goes to work just like Jesus did. Our experience of repentance has produced a revolutionary change in our feelings toward "every sinner." Of each one we genuinely feel, "There but for the grace of God am I!" Make no mistake about it: he will immediately sense the reality of our identity with him in exactly the same way that sinners sensed the reality of Christ's identity with them.

Why Only a Perfect Person Can Experience a Perfect Repentance

One more thought before we close this chapter. The more nearly perfect a person is, the greater will be his experience of repentance. Only a perfect Being can experience a perfect repentance. This is why only Christ is the perfect Example of corporate repentance.[1] Never before in world history and never since has a human being offered to the Father such a perfect offering of repentance in compensation for human sin. Because of His perfect innocence and sinlessness, only Christ could feel perfectly the weight of human guilt.

Ellen G. White has beautifully expressed this truth:

> Through Christ was man's only hope of restoration to the favor of God. Man had separated himself at such a distance from God by

---

[1] See excellent presentations of this idea in James Denney, *The Christian Doctrine of Reconciliation*, Hodder & Stoughton, London, 1917; McCleod Campbell, *The Nature of the Atonement*; R. C. Moberly, *Atonement and Personality*.

transgression of His law, that he could not humiliate himself before God proportionate to his grievous sin. The Son of God could fully understand the aggravating sins of the transgressor, and in His sinless character He alone could make an acceptable atonement for man in suffering the agonizing sense of His Father's displeasure. The sorrow and anguish of the Son of God for the sins of the world were proportionate to His divine excellence and purity, as well as to the magnitude of the offense. (*Selected Messages*, Book 1, pp. 283, 284.)

It is no accident, therefore, that only the 144,000 who are "without fault before the throne of God" (Revelation 14:5) will be able to approach unto Christ's perfect example of corporate repentance, although sinners by nature.

At every advance step in Christian experience our repentance will deepen. It is to those whom the Lord has forgiven, to those whom he acknowledges as His people, that He says, "Then shall ye remember your own evil ways, and your doings that were not good, and shall loathe yourselves in your own sight." Ezekiel 36:31. (*Christ's Object Lessons*, pp. 160, 161.)

Repentance is associated with faith, and is urged in the gospel as essential to salvation. ... There is no salvation without repentance. No impenitent sinner can believe with his heart unto righteousness, ...

As the sinner looks to the law, his guilt is made plain to him, and *pressed home to his conscience*, and he is condemned. His only comfort and hope is found in looking to the cross of Calvary. (*Selected Messages*, Book 1, pp. 365, 366.)

CHAPTER 5

HOW JESUS CALLED THE JEWS TO NATIONAL REPENTANCE

Fresh from His own experience of corporate repentance and baptism "in behalf of the human race," Jesus demanded repentance from the Jewish nation: "From that time Jesus began to preach and to say, Repent: for the kingdom of heaven is at hand." Matthew 4:17. The same call was echoed by the disciples: "And they went out, and preached that men should repent." Mark 6:12.

This call to repentance was the keynote of Jesus' ministry from beginning to end. His greatest disappointment was the refusal of the nation to respond. He upbraided "the cities wherein most of His mighty works were done, because they repented not." Matthew 11:20. The corporate nation of Israel was likened to the unfruitful "fig tree planted in His vineyard." "Behold, these three years I come seeking fruit on this fig tree, and find none." See Luke 13:6-9. What was the "fruit" Christ was seeking? Repentance.

The barren fig tree which Jesus cursed just before His final sufferings (Mark 11:12-14) became a symbol. It represented not the mere mass of individual unrepentant Jews, but the corporate people which as a nation rejected Christ:

> The cursing of the fig tree was an acted parable. That barren tree, flaunting its pretentious foliage in the very face of Christ, was a symbol of the Jewish nation. The Saviour desired to make plain to His disciples the cause and the certainty of Israel's doom. (*Desire of Ages*, p. 582.)

> Our Lord had sent out the twelve and afterward the seventy, proclaiming that the kingdom of God was at hand, and calling upon men to repent and believe the gospel. ... This was the message borne to the Jewish nation after the crucifixion of Christ; but the nation that claimed to be God's peculiar people rejected the gospel brought to them in the power of the Holy Spirit. (*Christ's Object Lessons*, p. 308.)

The leaders in the Jewish nation had signally failed of fulfilling God's purpose for His chosen people. Those whom the Lord had made a depositary of truth had proved unfaithful to their trust, and God chose others to do His work. (*Acts of The Apostles*, pp. 78, 79.)

The national sin of the Jewish people was accomplished through the action of the "religious leaders" which bound the nation to corporate ruin:

> When Christ came, presenting to the nation the claims of God, the priests and elders denied His right to interpose between them and the people. They would not accept His rebukes and warnings, and they set themselves to turn the people against Him and to compass His destruction.
>
> For the rejection of Christ, with the results that followed, they were responsible. A nation's sin and a nation's ruin were due to the religious leaders. (*Christ's Object Lessons*, pp. 304, 305.)

National Ruin Followed National Impenitence

It is obvious that only national repentance could have saved the Jewish nation from the impending ruin which their national sin invoked upon them:

> Paul showed that Christ had come to offer salvation first of all to the nation that was looking for the Messiah's coming as a consummation and glory of their national existence. But that nation had rejected Him who would have given them life, and had chosen another leader, whose reign would end in death. He endeavored to bring home to His hearers the fact that repentance alone could save the Jewish nation from impending ruin. (*Acts of The Apostles*, p. 247.)

Jesus last public discourse was a final appeal to the leaders of the nation at the Jerusalem headquarters to repent. Their refusal to do so called from Christ a heartbroken lament (see Matthew 23:13-37). With tears in His voice, the Saviour spoke of the national ruin impending: "All these things shall come upon this generation. O Jerusalem, Jerusalem ... !"

There is a distinct, difference between national repentance and personal repentance. He appealed to *individuals* to repent ("Joy shall be in heaven over one sinner that repenteth," Luke 15:7); and also appealed to "this wicked generation," that is, the nation ("The men of Nineve shall rise up in the judgement with this generation, and shall condemn it: for they repented at the preaching of Jonas," Luke 11:32).

Like a lone flash of lightning on a dark night, this reference to the "men of Nineve" illustrates Jesus' idea of national repentance. National repentance is such a rare thing that few believe the experience is even possible at any time. World history affords precious few examples, if any, with the phenomenal exception of the history of Nineveh,* Jesus used it as a ready example to prove that what He was calling for from the Jewish nation was not something practically impossible. If a heathen nation can repent, said Jesus in effect, surely the nation that claims to be God's chosen people can do the same!

> As Jonas was a sign unto the Ninevites, so shall also the Son of Man be to this generation. ... The men of Nineveh shall rise up in the judgement with this generation, and shall condemn it: for they repented at the preaching of Jonas; and behold, a greater than Jonas is here. (Luke 11:29-32.)

How Nineveh's Repentance Was Effected

If one picture is worth a thousand words, Nineveh's repentance is a sharply focused illustration of a national response to the call of God. The simple story as we find it in the Book of Jonah tells how a nation, not simply a scattered group of individuals, repented. Although we have never seen this happen in our day, there is no reason for us to doubt the truth of this sacred history. Let those who doubt that the Seventh-day Adventist Church can ever repent consider the history of heathen Nineveh!

It is easier for us moderns to believe that the "great fish" swallowed Jonah alive than to grasp the fact that a corporate nation did actually repent as a nation at the preaching of God's word, "The people of Nineveh believed God, and proclaimed a fast, and put on sackcloth, from the

---

* And possibly the Kingdom of Judah in the days of Josiah (2 Chronicles 34, 35). There may be unrecorded examples.

greatest of them even unto the least of them." Jonah 3:5. Amazing as it may seem to us, here is something that the "body" of a nation did!

Jonah goes on to explain how it was that this repentance began with "the greatest of them" and extended downward from the usual order in history to "the least of them." "For word came unto the King of Nineveh, and he arose from his throne, and he laid his robe from him, and covered him with sackcloth, and sat in ashes. *And he caused it to be proclaimed and published through Nineveh by the decree of the king and his nobles.*" Jonah 3:5-7.

Although the call to repent was not initiated at the royal palace, the government of Nineveh wholeheartedly supported it. The "city" repented from the "top" to the "bottom." If such an "exceeding great city" as a body "believed God, and proclaimed a fast, and put on sackcloth, from the greatest of them even unto the least of them," it is clear that the repentance was both nationally "proclaimed and published," and individually received. The divine warning had proclaimed a corporate "overthrow" of Nineveh as a city; the people's repentance was completely complementary. Jesus' point was that the fact that this happened once in history was proof that it could have happened in His day also.

Such a national repentance would have been very practical and easy to achieve. For it to have proceeded among the Jews as it did in ancient Nineveh "from the greatest of them even to the least of them" would have required that the High Priest, Caiphas, lead out. This he could have done had he simply accepted the principle of the cross.

How Caiphas Could Have Led Israel to Repentance

For example, even if he had sincerely not known how to relate himself to Jesus in the early days of the Saviour's ministry, he could at least at the time of Jesus' trial have taken a firm stand for the right. He could have said to the Sanhedrin members assembled, "For a long time I didn't understand the work of Jesus of Nazareth. You brethren have shared my misunderstanding. Something has been happening among us that has been beyond us. But I have been doing some study in the Scriptures lately. Now I have seen that beneath His lowly outward guise, Jesus of Nazareth is indeed the true Messiah. He fulfills the prophetic details. And now, brethren, I humbly acknowledge Him as such, and I forthwith step down from my high position and I shall be the first to install Him as Israel's true High Priest!"

A gasp of surprise would have run through the court chambers as Caiphas said these words. But had Caiphas done so, he would today be honored all over the world as the noblest leader of God's people in all history. The Jews, many of them, would doubtless have followed his lead, for we have already noted how their religious leaders fastened upon them their national guilt; thus it follows that they could also have led them into national repentance. Christ could have been "offered" in some other way than murder by His own people, and Jerusalem could today be the "joy of the whole earth" rather than its sorest plague spot.

The Jewish leaders, led by Caiphas, chose to reject Heaven's gift of corporate repentance. Terrible have been the sufferings of their children.

If it should be, through unmitigated tragedy, that the church of today should ultimately choose to follow ancient Israel in impenitence, Christ would suffer at her hands the most appalling humiliation He has ever had to endure. He would be crucified afresh, wounded anew "in the house of His friends." Humanity's final indignity would be heaped upon His sacrifice.

Fortunately, however, the very nature of His sacrifice on the cross assures us that the church will not at last repeat this tragic pattern of the past. For once in history, Christ will be fully vindicated by His professed people. An infinite price was paid for our redemption; in the end the great price will be seen to have been worthwhile. An infinite sacrifice will redeem and heal an almost infinite measure of impenitence.

"Certain of the scribes and Pharisees" approached Jesus as representatives of the nation, inquiring for evidence on which to base an official policy toward Him (Matthew 12:38). In reply He told them He would give them no further evidence than the divine call to repentance of which Jonah's call and ministry to Nineveh was an example. Accept Me as the Ninevites accepted Jonah, He said.

Though He was "a greater than Jonas" and "a greater than Solomon," yet He did not appear in the glorious garb and pomp of Solomon, nor did He "cause His voice to be heard in the streets" as did Jonah (cf. Matthew 12:41, 42; Isaiah 12:2). *But the Jewish leaders had evidence enough that Jesus was the true Messiah by the quality of His solemn call to repentance.* No other "sign" was to be given that "evil and adulterous generation." "The men of

Nineveh shall rise in Judgment with this generation and shall condemn it," literally at last, as well as figuratively in history. Israel's frightful doom was just, because they failed to recognize and heed Heaven's gracious call to repentance.

But still there remains a strange hope for ancient Israel's literal descendants in our day:

> I would not, brethren, that you should be ignorant of this mystery, lest ye should be wise in your own conceits; that blindness in part is happened to Israel, until the fulness of the Gentiles be come in. And so all Israel shall be saved. ... For the gifts and calling of God are without repentance. ... *Through your mercy they also may obtain mercy.* (Romans 11:25-31.)

The Ingathering of the Jews

The Spirit of Prophecy agrees with Paul's bright hope. In the days of the "loud cry" we shall see some surprising developments in regard to repentant Jews:

> When this gospel shall be presented in its fullness to the Jews, many will accept Christ as the Messiah. ...
>
> In the closing proclamation of the gospel, when special work is to be done for classes of people hitherto neglected, God expects His messengers to take particular interest in the Jewish people whom they find in all parts of the earth. ... This will be to many of the Jews as the dawn of a new creation, the resurrection of the soul. ... They will recognize Christ as the Saviour of the world. Many will by faith receive Christ as their redeemer. ...
>
> ... The God of Israel will bring this to pass in our day. His arm is not shortened that it cannot save. As His servants labor in faith for those who have long been neglected and despised, His salvation will be revealed. (*Acts of The Apostles*, pp. 380, 381.)

Could it be that these marvelous things have to wait only because of our continued impenitence? How can we possibly call Jews, even though they are "mighty in the scriptures," to such repentance unless we know the experience ourselves? God's great heart of pity is moved in behalf of the suffering Jews; and a great blessing is awaiting them when we are prepared to be the agents to bring it:

Notwithstanding the awful doom pronounced upon the Jews as a nation at the time of their rejection of Jesus of Nazareth, there have lived from age to age many noble, God-fearing Jewish men and women who have suffered in silence. God has comforted their hearts in affliction and has beheld with pity their terrible situation. He has heard the agonizing prayers of those who have sought Him with all the heart for a right understanding of His word. Some have learned to see in the lowly Nazarene whom their forefathers rejected and crucified, the true Messiah of Israel. As their minds have grasped the significance of the familiar prophecies so long obscured by tradition and misinterpretation, their hearts have been filled with gratitude to God for the unspeakable gift He bestows upon every human being who chooses to accept Christ as a personal Saviour. (*Ibid.*, pp. 379, 380).

One's heart beats a little faster when he reads those words so pregnant with hope and wonder. What joy to witness the fulfillment of Paul's bright visions of future restoration of the true Israel! Millions of sincere Christians of many denominations look to literal Israel in Palestine as the fulfillment; the servant of the Lord, in harmony with Paul's concept of justification by faith, foresaw the genuine.

Could it happen in our time?

Or must we all go into our graves and leave the blessing to a future generation to witness?

The repentance our Lord calls for from us is the key.

CHAPTER 6

HOW THE JEWISH NATION REJECTED REPENTANCE

Could Jesus accuse people of a crime when they were innocent?

If someone accused me, for example, of starting World War I, I would tell him that he was unreasonable. I wasn't even born when it started!

But Jesus accused the Jewish leaders of His day with responsibility and guilt for a crime committed 800 years before any of them were born. Under such circumstances, how could His hearers possibly be guilty? His charge against them sounds like one of the most fantastically irrelevant and unreasonable ever made.

The story is found in Matthew 23. Jesus has just finished upbraiding the scribes and Pharisees with a series of "woes" accompanied by vivid flashes of irony and indignation. There is no doubt that they were personally guilty of all the sins He catalogued in this series of "woes." He concludes in verse 34 with a prophecy that they would in future be guilty of even greater crimes, and then springs on them the charge of murdering a man 800 years *before they were born:*

> "That upon you may come all the righteous blood shed upon the earth, from the blood of righteous Abel unto the blood of Zacharias son of Barachias, whom ye slew between the temple and the altar" (verse 35).

For many years I read this verse assuming that this Zecahrias was a victim whom Christ's hearers had personally murdered in the temple during their lifetime. I took for granted that the crime must have taken place not more than 30 or 40 years previous.

Human Guilt from "A" to "Z"

It was a real shock to discover that this "Zacharias son of Barachias" was murdered in 856 B.C. (The story is recorded in 2 Chronicles 24:20, 21.)

Why did Jesus charge the responsibility and guilt of this crime upon the Jews of His day eight centuries after the real murderers had gone into their graves?

When we recognize the principle of corporate guilt, the picture becomes clear. Jesus was not being unfair. In hating Him, the Jewish leaders were merely acting out all human guilt from "A" to "Z," even though they may not as yet have personally committed a single act of murder. Jesus recognized that the Jewish leaders of His day were in spirit one corporate body with their "fathers" who had actually shed the blood of the innocent Zacharias in the temple.

Now, by refusing the call to repentance which John the Baptist and Jesus had sent them, they had chosen to retain the guilt of corporate involvement with all murders of innocent victims ever since the days of Cain and Abel. One who could not err fastened the entire load of guilt upon them.

Suppose the Jewish leaders had decided to repent? If so, they would have experienced a corporate repentance. They would have repented of "the blood of all the prophets, which was shed from the foundation of the world" (Luke. 11:50). This would have been a repentance appropriate to their guilt in hating and rejecting the Son of God.

This idea was deeply ingrained in Hebrew thinking. More than we may have supposed, the Hebrew pattern of thought regarding Israel and the church as a corporate personality makes sense to our modern minds.

It is one of Paul's dynamic ideas that the church is the "Isaac" of faith, "one body" with Abraham and all true believers of all ages. To Jewish and Gentile believers alike Paul represents Abraham as "our father" (Romans 4:1-13). Isaac is the "seed" (see Romans 9:6-33). To the Gentile believers Paul speaks of "our father: ... all baptized unto Moses," and adds, "we, being many are one bread, and one body" (see 1 Corinthians 10:1-17). "By one spirit are we all baptized into one body, whether we be Jews or Gentiles, whether we be bond or free; and have been all made to drink into one Spirit."

We "all" means exactly what the apostle says—"we all" are both past generations and the present generation. Christ's "body" is composed of all who have believed in Him from the time of Adam down to the last "remnant" who welcome Him at His second coining. All are "one" corporate individual in the pattern of Paul's Hebrew thinking. The moment we believe, we become a part of that "body" composed of the saints of all ages, each individual member as closely connected with all other members as the various organs of the human body, being separate, yet partake of one corporate unity.

How a Man Paid Tithe Even Before He Was Born

So deeply imbedded in Paul's mind was this Hebrew idea that he used a curious example to explain it. He said that Levi "paid tithes in Abraham." He was talking about the time when Abraham paid his tithes to Melchizedek, priest of the Most High God, and type of Christ. A little reflection will show that at the time Abraham paid these tithes following the battle of the vale of Siddim he as yet had no child at all. Levi was Abraham's great-grandson; yet Paul says that Levi paid tithes "in Abraham" *before even his own grandfather, Isaac, had been begotten!* "He was yet in the loins of his father (Abraham), when Melchizedec met him" (Hebrews 7:9, 10). Either Paul was seriously, even ludicrously, mistaken; or the Bible recognizes the principle of corporate identity "in Adam" and "in Christ."

The Corporate Personhood of Israel and the Church

Now let us see how the Old Testament further clarifies this idea:

(a) Speaking as a mouthpiece for the Lord, Hosea represents Israel through many generations of history as a single individual, stages in growth from birth through youth and adulthood. "When Israel was a child, then I loved him, and called my Son out of Egypt" (Hosea 11:1). Israel "shall sing there, as in the days of her youth, and as in the days when she came up out of the land of Egypt" (2:15). Israel as a nation is personified as a girl who is to become the wife of Israel's Lord.

(b) Ezekiel further develops the idea. He portrays the history of Jerusalem as an individual biography:

> Thus saith the Lord God unto Jerusalem: thy birth and thy nativity is of the land of Canaan; thy father was an Amorite, and thy mother an Hittite ... When I passed by thee, and looked upon thee, behold, thy time was the time of love. ... And thou wast exceedingly beautiful, and thou didst prosper into a kingdom. (Ezekiel 16:2-13).

Generations of Israelites may come and go, but the corporate personal identity remains. The guilt of "youth" is retained in adulthood as a person when an adult remains guilty of a wrong committed when he was a youth, even though the scientists say that every physical cell in his body has been replaced during intervening years. One's personal identity remains regardless of the molecular composition of his body. In Israel's case, their corporate guilt extended even to Calvary.

(c) Moses taught the same principle by projection into the future, addressing his generation as the "you" who should witness the fulfillment of his words in the ultimate captivity into Babylon which actually took place nearly a thousand years later (see Lev. 26:3-35).

(d) Moses also called upon succeeding generations to recognize and confess their corporate guilt with "their fathers:"

> If they shall confess their trespass which they trespassed against Me, and that they also have walked contrary to Me; and that I also have walked contrary unto them, and have brought them into the land of their enemies; if then their uncircumcised hearts be humbled, and they then accept the punishment of their iniquity ... I will for their sakes remember the covenant of their ancestors, whom I brought forth out of the land of Egypt. (Lev. 26:3-40).

They were explicitly to "confess their iniquity, and the iniquity of their fathers."

(e) Succeeding generations often recognized the truth of this principle. King Josiah, seeking to promote a corporate repentance in his day, confessed that "great is the wrath of the Lord that is kindled against us, because our fathers have not hearkened unto the words of this book, to do according unto all that which is written concerning us" (2 Kings 22:13). He said nothing about the guilt of his own generation, so clearly did he see their involvement with the guilt of previous generations. The writer of the Book of Chronicles agrees with this confession of corporate guilt (2 Chronicles 34:21).

(f) Ezra lumps together the guilt of his own generation with that of their fathers: "Since the days of our fathers have *we* been in a great trespass unto this day; and for *our* iniquities have we, our kings, and our priests, been delivered into the hand of the kings of the lands" (Ezra 9:7). "Our" kings" were those of previous generations, for there was no living king in Ezra's day.

(g) David writes his profound Psalms, experiencing in himself what Christ was to experience so perfectly that Christ actually used David's words to express the feelings of His own broken heart. "My

God, My God, why hast Thou forsaken Me?" the Saviour cries as He hangs upon His cross (Psalm 22:1; Matthew 27:46). The meditation and prayer of His stricken heart finds perfect expression in the experience of David. Christ is in fact the Hebrew Word "made flesh."

Nowhere is the perfect corporate identity of the "member" with the "Head" more clearly seen than in the David-Christ relationship. Christ knows Himself to be the "son of David." He has feasted upon David's words and been inspired by David's experiences. The perfect corporate identity He sees of Himself in the Old Testament, manifested through the experience and the words of the prophets, becomes lived out in His own flesh through faith.

(h) The Hebrew idea of identity reaches a zenith in the strange Song of Solomon. Here is the love story of the ages. Christ loves a "woman," even His church. Israel, the foolish "child" called out of Egypt, the fickle girl in her "time of love" in "youth," the faithless "wife" in the Kingdom days, "grieved and forsaken" in the Captivity, at last becomes the chastened and mature "bride" of Christ. At last she is prepared though perfect corporate repentance to become a mate to Him.

Someday soon, as soon as we really want it to be, it will be said, "The marriage of the Lamb is come, and His wife hath made herself ready" (Revelation 19:7).

A Demonstration of Corporate Repentance; Pentecost

Jesus was disappointed in His appeal to the Jews for a national repentance. Yet there did come in the experience of Pentecost a perfect demonstration of the *principle* of corporate repentance. At Pentecost the "remnant" who saw their sins as one with the sins of their "fathers" recognized their guilt of the blood of the Son of God. Peter charged them all with the same guilt: "Ye have crucified ... Christ" (Acts 2:36).

It is hardly likely that the "three thousand" who were converted that day were all personally present at Christ's trial and shouted "Crucify Him!" or mocked Him as He hung on the cross at Calvary. Peter's hearers at Pentecost recognized their guilt shared as a nation and as a people, even though they may not have personally taken part in murdering Christ. Repeatedly Peter laid the charge upon the leaders of the Jewish nation: "Be it known unto you all, and to all the people of Israel, that by the name of Jesus Christ of Nazareth, whom ye crucified, ... even by Him doth this man stand here before you whole" (Acts 4:10). Yet they stubbornly persisted in refusing to recognize their guilt. "Did not we straitly command you that ye should not teach in this name? ... Ye ... intend to bring this man's blood upon us" (Acts 5:28).

Peter was kind enough to concede that the people and their rulers did what they did "through ignorance;" but nevertheless, the guilt was laid where it belonged: "*Ye* denied the Holy One;" "*ye* delivered Him in the presence of Pilate; "*ye* ... desired a murderer to be granted unto you;" "*ye* ... killed the Prince of life" (Acts 3:13-15).

Pentecost was a glorious model and ideal inspiring God's people for nearly 2000 years. What made those grand results possible? *The people accepted the principle of corporate guilt, and frankly confessed their part in the greatest sin of all ages.* "When they heard this, they were pricked in their heart, and said unto Peter and to the rest of the apostles, Men and brethren, what shall we do?" (Acts 2:37).

The antithesis of Pentecost was the refusal of the Sanhedrin to accept Stephen's portrayal of corporate guilt through their national history. "Ye stiffnecked and uncircumcised in heart and ears, ye do always resist the Holy Ghost: as your fathers did, so do ye. Which of the prophets have not your fathers persecuted? and they have slain them which shewed before of the coming of the Just One; of whom ye have been now the betrayers and murderers" (Acts 7:51, 52). This was too much for these men. They "stopped their ears, and ran upon him with one accord, and cast him out of the city, and stoned him" (verses 57, 58).

A pattern had been worked out. It began with Cain, and extended throughout Israelite history. Generation after generation refused to acknowledge their corporate guilt. Israel earned her unique distinction to demonstrate to the world a tragic example of national impenitence, a solemn warning of the hopeless consequences of denominational pride and stubbornness. A similar ruin must overtake any church who follows her in impenitence.

But in that very hour when Israel sealed her eternal doom by murdering Stephen, a process began to work itself out in honest human nature that would lead to a corporate and national correction of the sin of Israel.

When the "witnesses laid down their clothes at a young man's feet, whose name was Saul," they little realized that this young man with a disturbed conscience would soon think through the structuring of a worldwide "body of Christ." It would eventually exhibit in full and final display the blessings of corporate and national repentance which the Jews tragically refused.

Ezekiel and Corporate Guilt

At this point, a sincere question needs to be considered: does Ezekiel deny the principle of corporate guilt and repentance? He says:

> What mean ye, that ye use this proverb, ... The fathers have eaten sour grapes, and the children's teeth are set on edge? ... Behold, all souls are Mine; as the soul of the father, so also the soul of the son is Mine: the soul that sinneth, it shall die. ...
>
> Yet ye say, Why? doth not the son bear the iniquity of the father? When the son hath done that which is lawful and right, and hath kept all My statutes, and hath done them, he shall surely live. The soul that sinneth it shall die. The son shall not bear the iniquity of the father, neither shall the father bear the iniquity of the son: the righteousness of the righteous shall be upon him, and the wickedness of the wicked shall be upon him. (Ezekiel 18:2, 4, 19, 20; cf. Jeremiah 31:29, 30).

Ezekiel discusses a good man who does everything right, but who has a son who does everything wrong. Then he discusses how the wicked man's son "seeth all his father's sins ... and doeth not such like." "He shall not die for the iniquity of his father" (verses 14-17). The prophet's point is that sin and guilt is not communicated genetically.

But Ezekiel surely doesn't intend to suggest that any "righteous" man is righteous of himself, nor does he intend to deny the Bible truth of justification by faith. Any "righteous" man must be righteous by faith, and apart from Christ he has no righteousness of his own. The "wicked" man is the one who rejects such righteousness by faith. The prophet does not deny that "all have sinned," and "all the world ... become guilty before God" (Romans 3:23, 19). Apart from the imputed righteousness of Christ, therefore, "all the world" is alike "guilty before God." Ezekiel is not denying the reality of corporate guilt which we all share "in Adam."

The "son" who saw his "father's sins" and repented is delivered from the guilt of those sins by virtue of Christ's righteousness, but he is not intrinsically better than his father. There is a certain sense in which his repentance is a corporate one: he realizes that had he been in his father's place he could well have been alike guilty. He does not think himself incapable of such sins. He humbly confesses, "There but for the grace of God am I."

Ellen White offers a challenging insight into the reality of corporate guilt and repentance:

> The life we live is to be one of continual repentance and humility. ... When we have true humility, we have victory. ... The mind is susceptible to divine impressions, and the light of God shines in, enlightening the understanding. ...
>
> A true sense of repentance before God does not hold us in bondage, causing us to feel like persons in a funeral procession. We are to be cheerful, not sorrowful. But all the time we are to be sorry that after Christ had given His precious life for us, we gave so many years of our life to the powers of darkness. ...
>
> As we see souls out of Christ, we are to put ourselves in their place, and in their behalf feel repentance before God, resting not until we bring them to repentance. If we do everything we can for them, and yet they do not repent, the sin lies at their own door; but we are still to feel sorrow of heart because of their condition, showing them how to repent, and trying to lead them step by step to Jesus Christ. (*MS* 92, 1901; *Seventh-day Adventist Bible Commentary*, Vol. 7, pp. 959, 960).

However faint such a reflection may be, repentance like this in "behalf" of others must be based on Christ's "repentance ... in behalf of the human race" that Ellen White discusses (*General Conference Bulletin*, 1901, p. 36). It would be impossible for any of us to feel such concern and sorrow "in behalf" of others, had He not felt it first in our "behalf."

If it is true that "we love because He first loved us," perhaps we can also say that we repent because He first repented in our "behalf." He is our Teacher. Let us be His disciples.

CHAPTER 7

CHRIST'S CALL TO THE CHURCH TO REPENT

The Spirit of Prophecy does not uphold the idea that the "saints" that "keep the commandments of God and the faith of Jesus" (Revelation 14:12) are some nondenominated and unorganized movement. While we know that some unconverted individuals in the church will eventually be "shaken out" in the final crisis, the denomination known as Seventh-day Adventists is recognized in the writings of Ellen G. White as the prophetic "remnant church," and the supreme object of the Lord's love:

> In a special sense Seventh-day Adventists have been set in the world as watchmen and light-bearers. To them has been intrusted the last warning for a perishing world, ... They have been given a work of the most solemn import,—the proclamation of the first, second, and third angels' messages. ...
>
> The most solemn truths ever intrusted to mortals have been given to us to proclaim to the world. The proclamation of these truths is to be our work. The world is to be warned, and God's people are to be true to the trust committed to them. (*Testimonies*, Vol. 9, p. 19.)

If the Seventh-day Adventist church has such a trust committed to her, it is equally true that Christ's message to Laodicea is addressed primarily to her rather than to Christendom in general, or to some splinter group within the church.* But notice that when Christ calls for repentance, He is speaking primarily not to the church at large, but to the leadership:

(1) The Book of Revelation is generally addressed "unto the seven churches," but the seven messages of chapters 2 and 3 are addressed particularly to the "*angels* of the seven churches." There is a reason for this distinction.

(2) The word "angel" means messenger (from *angellō*, to deliver a message), and can refer either to human or heavenly "messengers." (For

---

* See *Testimonies for the Church*, Vol. 1, pp. 186, 187; *Selected Messages*, Book 1, pp. 91-93; *Seventh-day Adventist Bible Commentary*, Vol. 7, pp. 959, 960, 961.

examples of *angelōs* used with reference to human beings see Matthew 11:10; Mark 1:2; Luke 7:24; 9:52.) The "angels of the seven churches" cannot be literal angels in heaven because these holy beings have neither left their "first love" nor "fallen" nor "suffered Jezebel to teach" nor lived a name when "dead" nor been "lukewarm." Neither do they have occasion to "repent." Christ directed John to write to the *human* leadership of the seven churches, in each instance a personified leadership addressed by the second person singular pronoun, "thou."

(3) Jesus Himself defines the "angels of the seven churches" as "the seven stars which thou sawest in My right hand." Revelation 1:16, 20. The Spirit of Prophecy, in turn, defines the "seven stars" for us: "God's ministers are symbolized by the seven stars." "Christ's ministers are the spiritual guardians of the people entrusted to their care." (*Gospel Workers*, pp. 13, 14.)

(4) In the case of the seventh church we recognize the church in the last period of the Christian era in the end of time as the same as the people of Revelation 12:17 and 14:12. The Seventh-day Adventist church is in a special, unique sense the church of Laodicea. It follows that the "angel of the church of the Laodiceans" is primarily the responsible leadership of the Seventh-day Adventist church. The "angel" includes all leadership on all conference levels and the local leadership of congregations, each segment or level appropriately responsible.

Note the following comments: "'Those things saith He that holdeth the seven stars in His right hand.' These words are spoken to the teachers in the church—those entrusted by God with weighty responsibilities." (*Acts of the Apostles*, page 586, emphasis added. Compare *Acts of the Apostles*, page 164, where "those whom God has appointed to bear the responsibilities of leadership" in the church are identified with "those in the offices that God has appointed for the leadership of His people.")

(5) The way Christ has dictated the Laodicean message proves that He respects the principles of church organization. He does not jump the lines of responsibility or go over the heads of leadership in order to appeal to the church at large. He intends that the "angel of the church" shall repent first; and then entrusts to that leadership the task of ministering the experience to the worldwide church. If this were not true, He would have addressed the message "to the church of the Laodiceans" and disregarded the "angel of the church." When Christ's plan is understood, and when His message is appreciated, far more quickly than

we suppose possible an experience of contrition and reconciliation with Christ will be communicated to the worldwide church, hearts will be humbled before the Lord, and a people will be prepared for the close of probation. There is no reason why this vast task cannot be accomplished within the lifetime of the readers of this book.

Will Christ Reject Laodicea?

The Laodicean message is full of hope for the church. It is loyal. It recognizes the church as Christ's one object of supreme regard. His appeal to repent means clearly that He entertains infinite hope of success, that He fully expects His church to respond, else He would not waste His effort. His call expresses confidence in His church. Further, the time lapse of well over a century indicates His patience and long-suffering which He could not bestow upon an object which He intended ultimately to abandon.

Some are tempted to discouragement by the words, "Because thou art lukewarm ... I will spew thee out of My mouth" (Revelation 3:16). They feel that the church is so enfeebled and defective that Christ has either already fulfilled this promise and actually "spued" her out of His mouth, that is, rejected her; or that He will soon do so. In other words, they feel that the church is doomed, and this doom is just as sure and certain as is the fact that she is lukewarm. They add, "The Lord has made a definite promise; the church is lukewarm; therefore, the 'spewing out' is only a matter of time, or perhaps already accomplished."

The original language makes clear that Jesus did not say that He would indeed "spew out" His lukewarm church. What He said was, "I am about to spew thee out of My mouth" (*mellō se emesai*). Since the apostle John wrote both the Revelation and the Gospel bearing his name, we can better understand this expression by seeing how he used the same word *mellō* ("I am *about* to") in another passage. Speaking of the "nobleman whose son was sick at Capernaum," John says that the son "was *at the point of death*" (John 4:47), using *mellō*. What he says in plain English is that the boy was critically ill, about to die, *but did not die.*

What Jesus says to us in plain English is, "I am suffering acute nausea on account of your lukewarmness," or, "you make Me sick." He does not say that the spewing out is inevitable. Rather, He begs His church to "heal" His "nausea" by the only means practicable: "Be zealous, therefore, and repent."

In our denominational history movements have occasionally arisen on the assumption that Christ has already "spewed out" the leadership of His church. These result from a general misunderstanding of His call to repent. It is assumed (1) that the call to repent is for individual repentance; (2) that it has been understood; and (3) that it has been rejected. This essay presents evidence that (1) the call is to corporate and denominational repentance; (2) it has not been fully understood; and (3) it has, therefore, not been rejected, at least not finally.

If it should eventually be that Christ's call is finally rejected, the "I am about to spew thee out" would of course become "I have spewed thee out." But that great "if" is not true. It would require the failure of the Laodicean message and the final defeat of the Lord Jesus as faithful Divine lover. Everyone who is willing to concede such a defeat for Christ makes clear that he stands on the side of Satan, for Satan is determined that such a defeat must take place. Even the nagging doubt that expresses the "if" is born of unbelief. It is Satan that constantly assailed the Son of God with those barbed "ifs": "*If* Thou be the Son of God," "*if* ... Thou worship me"; and at the cross, "*if* He be the King of Israel," "*if* God will have Him." We are on Satan's side in the great struggle if we talk about "*if* the Bride repents and makes herself ready," or "*if* the church responds." That doubt of Christ's complete vindication paralyzes our devotion like nerve gas paralyzes a person's will.

The Remedy for Laodicea's Problems

Since Christ's call to repent is sent to the angel of the church, its human leadership, with the intent that the experience be ministered to the church at large, it is clear He calls for a corporate and denominational repentance.

It is denominational pride and complacency which is rebuked in the message of the True Witness. Therefore, the remedy proposed is denominational repentance. The medicine must fit the disease.

Therefore, we miss the point of the Laodicean message when we assume that the call to repent is merely for personal sin. it is true that we all as individuals have sins and weaknesses for which we should repent. For example, we may battle for the victory over an evil temper, perverted appetite, love of amusement, pride of dress, or sensuality. An infinite list of personal sins could be compiled. But the point of the Lord's appeal in Revelation 3 is that as a church and, more particularly as church leadership, we are guilty of denominational sin.

This sin is specifically (1) denominational pride ("Thou sayest, I am rich and I have been enriched"); (2) denominational complacency ("Thou sayest, I have need of nothing"); (3) denominational self-deception ("Thou knowest not that thou art wretched"); and (4) denominational assumptions of success which are not divinely validated ("Thou art miserable, and poor, and blind, and naked").

The remedies proposed are for the healing of these denominational ills: "gold tried in the fire," "white raiment," and "eyesalve." To the leadership of the church the Lord Jesus says, "As many as I love, I rebuke and chasten: be zealous therefore, and repent." Upon the minds of church leadership there is deeply impressed as never before in world history a sense of the Lord's love for the corporate body of His last-day church, a love that finds expression not in pampering denominational pride but in "faithful and true" rebuke and chastening, albeit with abundant evidence of loyalty.

We Must Succeed Where the Jews Failed

There is no difficulty in understanding what the Lord Jesus means by His call to repentance. We have a divine illustration of it in His call to the leadership of the Jewish nation of His day. If we find out what He meant then, we know what He means now. With the repentance of Nineveh standing in sacred history as the model, we can easily see the pattern that the Lord Jesus expects to see develop today. "From the greatest of them to the least of them," the repentance envisaged in the Laodicean message must spread from the "top to the bottom" throughout the worldwide church. When the experience Christ calls for is understood and embraced by the "angel" of the church, the methods of its promotion will be. uniquely effective. It will be clearly seen that the Holy Spirit, not advertising promotional technique, will have "caused it to be proclaimed and published." As in Nineveh's day, "the king and his nobles" will range themselves solidly in support of the experience Christ calls for. (See Jonah 3:5-9).

Where the Jews of Christ's day failed, "the angel of the church of the Laodiceans" is to succeed. Although it is true that in past history God's calls to repentance have usually been refused, it is not necessary to expect that the final call He sends to the last-day church must also fail. The prophetic picture is clear that something must happen in the end of time that has never happened before. The long sad history of milleniums of defeat must be changed at last, and the remnant church glorify the Lord and vindicate Him before the world and before the universe in a way that has never yet been done. Thus the church will "make herself ready" to be worthy to become the Bride of Christ. Doesn't Christ deserve this? Hasn't He sacrificed enough and suffered enough that at last His church shall give Him the kind of complete surrender that a bride gives to her husband? Doesn't Calvary demand such a response from us? Should it be any longer delayed?

Success Not Only Possible, But Certain

Nothing could be more tragic in the end of history than for a disappointed Christ to have to stand before "the door" knocking in vain and ultimately turning away in the sadness of defeat. But the picture we see in Revelation 3:20 and 21 indicates complete success.

Christ purchased the church of God with His own blood (Acts 20:28), and thus richly deserves from her this full measure of devotion. Surely this will be the experience of Jesus' "bride." "The sacrifices of God are a broken spirit: a broken and a contrite heart, O God, Thou will not despise" (Psalm 51:17). By virtue of the infinte sacrifice on Calvary, let us have confidence that the Laodicean message will fully accomplish its objective.

The fact that the Jews failed does not mean that modern Israel must also fail:

> That which Cod purposed to do for the world through Israel, the chosen nation, He will finally accomplish through His church on earth today. He has "let out His vineyard to other husbandmen," even to His covenant-keeping people, who faithfully "render Him the fruits in their season." (*Prophets and Kings*, pp. 713, 714.)

How encouraging this prophecy is! Lessons *can* be learned. The impenitent "old Jerusalem" will become the penitent "New Jerusalem," both corporate bodies. The transformation from the one to the other will be accomplished through the power of divine love.

Critics of the church who have given up hope and expect ultimate corporate failure mark her inward defects. They cannot see how God's love could possibly be loyal to such a faulty, erring church. Their mistake is a failure to discern the true nature of love. They assume, perhaps innocently, that divine love is like human love. Human love is conditioned and dependant on the value or virtue of its object. We "fall in love" with someone beautiful or wonderful. We cannot comprehend falling in love with someone ugly or evil. So critics look at the enfeebled and defective condition of the church and wonder how God's love for her can be permanent. "The church has failed," they say; "therefore, God's patient love must cease." What they have not yet seen is that divine love, being free and sovereign, is not dependent on the goodness or value of its object. *It creates goodness and value in its object.*

It is this creative quality of divine love which assures the complete success of the message of "the faithful and true witness" to the "angel of the church of the Laodiceans."

The Laodicean church is the "new covenant" church. Not for her own intrinsic goodness nor for her "works" will the Lord remain loyal to her, but because He remains a covenant-keeping God. "Not for thy righteousness, or for the uprightness of thine heart, dost thou go to possess their land: but ... that the Lord thy God ... may perform the word which the Lord sware unto thy fathers, Abraham, Isaac, and Jacob" (Deuteronomy 9:5). For the honor and glory of His name He will remain loyal to His church and in her vindication before the world Christ too will be vindicated. His sacrificial love will be proven justified.

Perhaps enough has been said in this chapter already. But we should consider one more question before we finish. Is it our business to ask whether an experience of corporate or denominational repentance is necessary, practical, or even beneficial?

We have no right to sit in judgment on our Lord's call and deliberate over its value as though it were a human suggestion someone makes. Perish the very thought that we have any right to reject it! Is He not our Lord and Master? Did He not give His blood for us? Is it not sufficient that the Lord Jesus Christ calls for repentance? How dares anyone to say, "Well, I like the idea, but I doubt it will work," or, "In my opinion, we're not all that bad that we need denominational repentance." No committee or council can contradict Christ's call.

The universe of heaven is watching us on their equivalent of TV. They watched the crucifixion of the Prince of glory. They have seen that He has called for a humbling of heart, contrition, melting of soul, from the denomination that prides itself on being the "remnant church."

What response will they see us make in this our generation?

CHAPTER 8

HOW CAN A CHURCH OF MILLIONS OF MEMBERS REPENT?

The assumption held by many for decades is that Christ's call to Laodicea to repent is addressed to individuals alone, whose problems are confined to miscellaneous personal failings. We don't deny that the call includes individuals; the point is that it embraces much more.

It has become obvious that His call is to "the *angel* of the church" in the true Biblical sense of a body. Immediately therefore the question arises, Is it possible for an organized body to repent? Does increasingly complex organization get in the way of the Holy Spirit's true work on earth? Must the "body" on earth become more disjointed and uncoordinated, like a quadriplegic patient whose spasms and jerks are uncontrollable by the head? We believe that the Bible has an answer that is clearly understandable in the light of history.

The essential quality of repentance remains the same in all ages and in all circumstances. People, not machines, not organizations, repent. But the repentance called for from Laodicea is unique in circumstances, depth, and extent. The church is not a machine, nor is its organization impersonal. The church is a body, and its organization is its vital functioning capacity. The individuals comprising this body can repent as a body.

As we have seen, *metanoia* (Greek for repentance) is literally perceptive "afterthought." It cannot be complete until the close of history, nor can it be complete until corporate guilt is discerned. So long as a "tomorrow" may provide further reflection on the meaning of our "mind" today, or so long as another's sins may yet disclose to us our own deeper guilt, our repentance must be incomplete.

But it will grow. Ellen G. White offers this perceptive insight into the ever-deepening experience that repentance is:

> At every advance step in Christian experience our repentance will deepen. It is to those whom the Lord has forgiven, to those whom He acknowledges as His people, that He says, 'then shall ye remember your own evil ways, and your doings that were not good, and shall loathe yourselves in your own sight.' Again He. says, 'I will establish My covenant with thee, and thou shalt know that I am the

Lord; that thou mayest remember, and be confounded, and never open thy mouth any more because of thy shame, when I am pacified toward thee for all that thou hast done, saith the Lord God.' Then our lips will not be opened in self-glorification. We shall know that our sufficiency is in Christ alone. (*Christ's Object Lessons*, pp. 160, 161.)

A Bright Future for God's Work

A most beautiful experience is on the "program" of coming events, an experience unique in history. Zechariah, Christ-centered prophet of last-day events, tells us that there will come to the denominated church and its leadership a heart-response to Calvary that will completely transform, the church. Speaking of the final events, the prophet says:

> And I will pour upon the house of David, and upon the inhabitants of Jerusalem, the spirit of grace and of supplications: and they shall look upon Me whom they have pierced, and they shall mourn for Him, as one mourneth for his only son, and shall be in bitterness for Him as one is in bitterness for his firstborn ... In that day there shall be a fountain opened to the house of David and to the inhabitants of Jerusalem for sin and for uncleanness. (Zechariah 12:10 -13:1.)

Who are "the inhabitants of Jerusalem"? Clearly, the members of Christ's church. Jerusalem is a "city," a symbol of the nation of Abraham's descendants, the organized body of God's people. In Zechariah's day, "Jerusalem" was the word that denominated as distinct before the world that particular group of people who were called to represent the Lord to the nations of the world. Jerusalem was a corporate, denominated, organized body of professed worshippers. She had just completed seventy years of disintegration and exile as punishment for centuries of rebellion and apostasy. Now the prophet, has been called to predict her reconstitution and reinstatement as the denominated people who will again represent Jehovah to the nations of earth. "The spirit of grace and supplications" is not to be poured out on scattered individual descendants of Abraham invisibly connected by mutual faith, but on the inhabitants of the "city," a visible body of God's denominated people on earth. In the setting of Zechariah's prophecy, it is implied that no descendant of Abraham choosing to dwell outside "Jerusalem" will share in the outpouring of the "spirit of grace and supplications." And we do know that those Jews were "lost" to history who chose to remain in the nations where they were scattered, refusing to move back to the ancestral nation in Palestine.

Who are "the house of David"? Obviously not Christ Himself, for "the house of David" share with "the inhabitants of Jerusalem" the guilt of "piercing" Christ. As it was the "house of David" that was anciently the government of the denominated people of God, it seems reasonable to conclude that the term refers to the leadership of the last-day church or "the angel of the church." "The house of David" are "the king and his nobles," to borrow Jonah's terminology regarding the city of Nineveh. They are "the men of Judah" whom Daniel speaks of in distinction to "the inhabitants of Jerusalem" (Daniel 10:7), Judah being the reigning tribe of the nation. "The house of David" includes all levels of leadership in the organized remnant church. Every community served by a congregation is a microcosm of the world, and the church there is its "Jerusalem." To the world itself, the world church is its "Jerusalem," its world leadership, "the house of David" designated to receive "the spirit of grace and supplications."

Does it seem fantastic that such a "spirit" shall be poured out on a body of leadership congested by organizational complexity? The more complex the church becomes, the more involved its multitudinous departments, the greater is the danger of the collective self of its large organization choking the simple, direct promptings of the Holy Spirit. Each individual catching a vision is tempted to feel that "his hands are tied"—what can he do? The great organizational monolith, permeated with pride and lukewarmness, seems to move only at an agonizing snail pace. Aside from this "spirit of grace and supplications," the nearer we come to the end of time, the bigger the church becomes, the more complex and congested are its movement, the more remote appears the prospect of accomplishing its worldwide task.

Why the Organization is Needed

Zechariah's prophecy calls for denominational repentance as the only possible remedy. The world needs a "Jerusalem" as a "witness to all nations." Without "Jerusalem" the task cannot be done. The history of the failure of old Jerusalem proves that without "the spirit of grace and of supplications," denominational organization inevitably becomes proud and misrepresentative of its divine mission. Zechariah says that the sense of contrition that a correct view of Calvary imparts ("they shall look on Me whom *they* [not the Jews and Romans of a past millenium] have pierced") will provide the ultimate solution to the problem of human "sin and uncleanness."

What is "the spirit of grace and supplications" poured out on the church and its leadership? Two distinct elements make up this phenomenal experience: "the spirit of grace," an appreciation of God's grace, a view of His character of love completely devastating and annihilating to human self-sufficiency and pride; and "the spirit of supplications," prayers arising from broken, contrite hearts. The difference in essential quality between these prayers and formal ordinary petitions is very great. Sinners will immediately detect the genuineness of these "supplications" because they will come from hearts transformed by corporate repentance. When prayer comes from a heart broken in contrition, "then will I teach transgressors Thy ways; and sinners shall be converted unto Thee" (Psalm 51:13).

The spirit of worship and service pervading every congregation will be immediately recognized. In close context to Zechariah's prophecy of chapter 10, we find another prophecy showing what could be the soul-winning results of such denominational repentance:

> People from around the world will come on pilgrimages and pour into Jerusalem from many foreign cities to attend these celebrations. People will write their friends in other cities [denominations] and say, "Let's go to Jerusalem to ask the Lord to bless us, and be merciful to us. I'm going! Please come with me. Let's go *now!*" (Zechariah 8:20, 21, *Living Prophecies*, paraphrased by Kenneth N. Taylor.)

The Cross and Denominational Repentance

How will this precious "spirit of grace and supplications" be poured out? What can we possibly do to hasten the fulfillment of this prophecy? Must we go into our graves as have previous generations and leave this marvelous experience to await some future generation? If we refuse the experience of repentance Christ calls for, yes. If we hold to "business-as-usual" pride and dignity, yes. If we permit past patterns of denominational reaction to continue, yes.

The answer to the question "how?" is the cross. "They shall look on

Me whom *they* have pierced," the Lord says. *Here is the full recognition of corporate guilt;* and the "spirit" bestowed follows the full, frank experience of corporate repentance. All human sin centers in the murder of the Son of God. So long as this is not perceived, the "spirit of grace and supplications" is unwelcome to the proud heart and, therefore, not receivable. We remain like little children contentedly unaware of our true spiritual condition. A knowledge of the full truth brings deep sorrow for sin, not a self-centered fear of punishment, but a Christ-centered sympathy for Him in His sufferings.

This transfer of concern from self to Christ is the most miraculous aspect of this amazing development among God's people. "They shall mourn *for Him*, as one mourneth for his only son, and shall be in bitterness for Him, as one that is in bitterness for his firstborn [that dies]" (Zechariah 12:10). To shift the focus of concern in the hearts of God's people from anxiety regarding their own eternal salvation to such sympathy for Christ—this is absolutely astounding. Were there no power of the Holy Spirit to accomplish the miracle, we might in our human judgment estimate that many decades would be necessary to effect such a change in human nature.

Zechariah goes on to describe how this heart sympathy for Christ will move the people. Taylor seems to have caught the idea;

> The sorrow and mourning in Jerusalem at that time will be even greater than the grievous mourning for the godly king Josiah, who was killed in the valley of Megiddo. All of Israel will weep in profound sorrow. The whole nation will be bowed down with universal grief—king, prophet, priest, and people. Each family will go into private mourning, husband and wife apart, to face their sorrow alone. (Zechariah 12:11-14, *Living Prophecies.*)

Such "repentance" can be nothing less than receiving the "mind of Christ." The last church is composed of individuals who, like everyone else in human history, were born with a "reprobate mind," the natural unregenerate heart of the sinner. But for them the transformation of "mind" will be complete. The more fully the "mind of Christ" is received, the deeper becomes their sense of contrition. The after-perception of the enlightened mind views sin without illusion.

Nevertheless, deep repentance is the very opposite of despair or gloominess. Only when one can view his sinful state with the repentance of such enlightened "after-perception" can he begin to appreciate the "good news" Christ proclaims. Those who fear repentance lest it induce gloom or sadness misunderstand the "mind of Christ" and close their eyes to the healing power of the Holy Spirit. The cheerfulness of the world is superficial and quickly turns to despair under severe trial. "Not as the world giveth" is the joy of Christ which is consistent with the fact that He was "a man of sorrows and acquainted with grief." As the remnant church ministers amidst the tragic disintegration of human life that more and more characterizes these last days, she needs that deep unfailing "joy of the Lord" that can come only from a deep experience of repentance and contrition. We cannot truly "believe the good news" as Jesus wants us to until we truly "repent" as He calls us to do.

Repentance for the *individual* is the perceptive after-thought that views personal character in the light of Calvary. What was previously unconscious becomes open to perception and understanding. The deep-seated sin of the soul, the corruption of the motives, all are viewed in the light that streams from the cross. As taught in the New Testament, repentance and faith are interwoven with the experience of appreciation of the atonement.

Repentance for the *church body* is the perceptive after-thought that views denominational history from the perspective of Calvary. What was previously unconscious within history becomes open. Movements and developments that were mysterious at the time are seen in their larger, truer significance. As with individual repentance, an experience of corporate repentance is possible only when the meaning of faith is clearly appreciated .

Pentecost forever defines the glorious reality of repentance. No one could fully grasp what repentance meant until after the cross. Mincing no words, Peter laid the full guilt of Christ's murder on his hearers: "Therefore, let all the house of Israel know assuredly, that God hath made that same Jesus whom ye have crucified, both Lord and Christ" (Acts 2:36). The result of this bold proclamation was an experience that was phenomenal, a human response never before (and seldom since) seen: "When they heard this, they were pricked in their heart, and said unto Peter and to the rest of the apostles, Men and brethren, what shall we do?" (verse 37). The events of verses 41 through 47 are glorious. Having experienced the depths of contrition, the early church was prepared to experience the heights of joyful, ministering love.

The "Why" of Apostolic Success

This syndrome of "ye crucified Christ/therefore repent ye" was the basis for the success of the early church. "Christ crucified" became the central appeal of all the apostles' ministry. Their hearers had no illusions about where the guilt lay. The Book of Acts would have been impossible unless every converted member of the early church realized his full share of the corporate guilt of that generation (as of all previous generations) in the murder of the Son of God, and likewise shared in the joyful experience of appropriate repentance.

From Acts 10 onwards we read of how others beside Jews partook of the same glorious experience. Yet the Gentiles had no personal share in the events of Calvary. The apostles are said to have marvelled that the Gentiles should experience the same phenomenal response to the cross that the believing Jews did, and thus receive the gift of the Holy Spirit (Acts 10:44-47). Peter and his followers evidently did not expect this response, because Peter was careful in his sermon in Cornelius's home to tell the Gentiles that it was *the Jews* who "slew and hanged [Christ] on a tree." He said nothing about the Gentiles being guilty. The phenomenal reception of the Holy Spirit was due to the believing Jew's phenomenal repentance for the sin of the ages—crucifying the Son of God. How could the "innocent" Gentiles share in this experience?

The Holy Spirit sent His words closer home than Peter expected. *His contrite hearers identified themselves with the Jews and recognized themselves as fully sharing in the guilt.* Only thus could they have shared the depths of repentance which made possible their reception of the power of the Holy spirit. In other words, they experienced corporate repentance.

Nothing in Scripture indicates that the reception of the Holy Spirit in the last days will be any different.

Everywhere Paul went among Jews and Gentiles, he "determined not to know anything among you, save Jesus Christ and Him crucified" (1 Corinthians 2:2). He brought His hearers to the scene of the crucifixion. He reminded his Galatian converts that "Jesus Christ hath been evidently set forth, crucified among you" (Galatians 3:1). He made them attend the proceedings that Friday.

Would You Have Done Better?

Let us try to picture ourselves as one of the crowd that gathered before Pilate that Friday morning. The strange Prisoner stands bound. It is popular to join in condemning Him. Not a voice is raised in His defense.

Suppose you are connected with Pilate's government, or are in the employ of Caiphas, the High Priest. Would you have the courage to stand up alone before that crowd and say, "We are making a terrible mistake here. This man is not guilty of these charges. He is indeed what He claims to be—He is the divine Son of God! I appeal to you, Pilate and Caiphas, don't condemn this Man"? While it is true that Pilate's wife sent him a private note making such an appeal, based on her dream, not one person dared to make a public appeal in Christ's behalf.

Suppose your job depended on the favor of these rulers. Suppose your own close circle of friends have already joined the mockery and abuse of Jesus—would you (or I) have the nerve to face them and rebuke them for what they do?

Realizing how easily your defense of Jesus might put you on the cross, too, would you (or I) have dared to speak out?

"The whole world stands charged today with the deliberate rejection and murder of the Son of God." "Upon all rests the guilt of crucifying the Son of God."

When this universal guilt is clearly sensed by human hearts, and God's forgiveness truly appreciated, Pentecost will be repeated. We dare not say that the church as a body cannot know this repentance, lest when we survey the wondrous cross on which the Prince of glory died, we pour contempt on His loving sacrifice by implying that it was in vain.

CHAPTER 9

CORPORATE REPENTANCE AND OUR DENOMINATIONAL HISTORY

Is there a special reason why our Lord calls the "remnant church" to repent? This serious question deserves a careful answer.

It is easy to assume that only false or apostate churches need to repent. (The fact is that as corporate bodies they are beyond it). The more convinced we are that a certain denomination represents the true "remnant church" of Bible prophecy, the more perplexed we are to understand how she seriously needs an experience of repentance. But her only hope lies in that possibility.

There is objective evidence that the Seventh-day Adventist church is the people symbolized by the "remnant." Her basic, unique doctrines are taken strictly from Holy Scripture. She establishes her identity by pinpoint accuracy of historical fulfillment of the prophecies of the rise of the "remnant" in the time of the end (Revelation 12:1-17). She is bearing to the world the three angels' messages that prophecy says will be the task of the last-day church (see Revelation 14:1-14). She evidences that she is the heir of those who throughout history have held to the simplicity and purity of apostolic faith.

> Do not these words (Exodus 31:12-17) point us out as God's denominated people? and do they not declare to us that so long as time shall last, we are to cherish the sacred, denominational distinction placed upon us? ...
>
> In a special sense Seventh-day Adventists have been set in the world as watchmen and light-bearers. To them has been entrusted the last warning for a perishing world. On them is shining wonderful light from the word of God. They have been given a work of the most solemn import,—the proclamation of the first, second, and third angels' messages. There is no other work of so great importance. ...
>
> The most solemn truths ever entrusted to mortals have been given us to proclaim to the world. The proclamation of these truths is to be our work. The world is to be warned, and God's people are to be true to the trust committed to them. (*Testimonies*, Vol. 9, pp. 18, 19.)

To be such a denominated people, to make such a claim to mankind—is it any wonder that corporate pride can easily arise in our hearts? And, of course, pride always resists any call to repentance. This has ever been true since the inception of Israel.

No one would be so foolish as to deny that individuals in the church need to repent. The problem arises when the Lord's call to "the angel of the church" is understood to apply to the church as a *body*, and especially its leadership.

Does our denominational history support Christ's call to denominational repentance? There are several possible ways of looking at our history:

(1) We can view it with corporate pride and satisfaction as does a sports team that has never lost a game. It's great to be on the winning side. This attitude interprets God's blessings on the church as His vindication and approval. Current denominational history is interpreted as "progress" or as "advance." Objective evaluation of the "progress" becomes rare. The result of this attitude is lukewarmness. It is by far the most popular view of our history, but it generates an unchristlike spiritual arrogance, the opposite of New Testament faith.

(2) Others view our history with despair, interpreting our real failures as evidence that the Lord has cast off this denomination and forsaken it. This view has produced various offshoots from time to time, and continually spawns new movements of fruitless, destructive criticism. Often these movements are initiated as a legitimate protest against, although they seldom offer a practical solution to the problem.

Both groups strenuously oppose the principle of denominational repentance, the first on the grounds that it is *unnecessary* since "all is well." To suggest that it is necessary is regarded as impertinent, even disloyal, as the ancient priests regarded Jeremiah's appeals. The second group reject it on the grounds that it is *impossible*, since they assume that the Lord has withdrawn from the church both the privilege and the possibility of repentance.

(3) We can view our history with firm confidence that this is the true "remnant" of prophecy and that God has led and overruled, but with a keen sense of contrition and humility in view of our failure to honor our Lord as prophecy indicates must be done. The world has not yet truly been made conscious of the message, and His people have not been prepared for the second coming of Jesus Christ. This view "rejoiceth in

the truth." It does not seek to evade or suppress the obvious facts of denominational history that call for humbling of heart and repentance. Nevertheless, *it is a view highlighted with hope.*

Attempts to Explain the Long Delay

Truth always gives ground for hope; and truth always accompanies the crucifixion of self, the antithesis of human pride. But human pride uncorrected, without repentance, will succeed in destroying any ground of hope and cause large numbers of discouraged church members to lose their way eventually. The "all is well" syndrome leads inevitably to frustrated despair for the simple reason that one's sober judgment insists that all is not well. In view of the needs of the world and the comparative impotence of God's people, such pride is seen to be a form of self-hypnosis.

The blindest Laodicean is forced to recognize that the long delay in the fruition of the pioneers' hopes has to be explained in some way. Something somewhere has to "give." The natural consequence of this perplexity is a variety of suggestions as to *what* must "give":

(a) Disloyal critics and offshoots consistently declare that the integrity of the church itself must "give," that is, its hopes are disappointed simply because its very existence has become illegitimate. It has forfeited the favor of God and no longer represents a valid movement of His leading. The church is Babylon, they say, its leadership an apostate hierarchy no better in principle than the Roman hierarchy. This of course is an extreme reaction against denominational pride and arrogance.

(b) Increasingly attractive to intellectual circles is the position that it is the fundamental doctrines of the church that must "give." The pioneers, they say, were theologically naive. In particular, the sanctuary doctrine that made the Advent Movement a unique denomination is in no way supported by Scripture. The entire 1844 doctrine and experience is assumed to be a sham. Again, this "solution" is a consequence of impenitence. The entertainment of Laodicean pride eventually results in the total disintegration of the denominational fabric.

(c) At this writing, widespread propaganda suggests that it is also our historic understanding of the Spirit of Prophecy that must "give." Ellen White did not enjoy the extent of divine inspiration that we have thought was the case. She was inspired only in the sense that countless other religious writers of influence in the evangelical world have been inspired. (Of course, this position makes her out to be a liar, for she claimed direct prophetic inspiration—but something must "give," and the carnal heart having long resented Ellen White's high Christlike standards, destroying her true prophetic credibility meets with a surprising degree of acceptance.)

All attempts to validate our sanctuary and prophetic doctrines on the authority of Ellen White (assuming that these doctrines are not biblical) are vain, because side by side with the debunking of our foundational doctrines as unbiblical comes the attempt also to debunk Ellen White herself. Those who question the Scriptural basis of our doctrines are usually equally ready to question Ellen White's authority.

(d) Implicit in these proposed explanations of the long delay lurks a virtual charge against God Himself. "My Lord delayeth His coming" is the contrapuntal theme. From the days of the pioneers, He has mocked the prayers of a sincere people who have been loyal to His commandments against the ridicule and resistance of the Christian world. He has callously disappointed them, not only on October 22, 1844, but continually ever since, permitting sincere, prayerful pioneers and their followers to misunderstand the prophecies of Daniel and the letter to the Hebrews. While they have valiantly sought to refute their opponents who would deny the basis of their faith, all the while the Lord has upheld their opponents theologically and permitted His commandment-keeping people to be naively blind.

If the Lord has not actually given it to them, He has at least permitted His Sabbath-keeping people to drink the bitter cup of shame and humiliation before the Christain world. There are even respected voices that now suggest that the basic doctrine of the personal, literal, visible second coming of Christ must "give." The descent of the Holy Spirit at Pentecost was the real second coming, and it has been going on ever since. How cruel the Lord must be for over a century to permit a people loyal to Him to be so deceived! How could Seventh-day Adventists continue to trust the Deity as a loving, personal Heavenly Father? When self-denying pioneers earnestly begged Him for bread, He gave them a theological stone. They were so naive that they thought the Bible meant what it says in plain language, supposing that the common man could understand it.

Christ's Solution to Our Denominational Impasse

(e) If Christ's call to "the angel of the church of the Laodiceans" is understood as a call to denominational repentance, then it is obvious that (1) the integrity of the church remains intact as the true "remnant" (2) its foundational doctrines are valid and thoroughly Scriptural; (3) Ellen White remains, despite criticism and attacks, a true, honest agent who exercised the gift of the spirit of prophecy; (4) the Lord has not delayed His coming nor has He mocked the sincere prayers of His people who have been loyal to His law. The pioneers were led of the Holy Spirit in their understanding of the prophecies and of the sanctuary doctrine.

What must "give" then, is *our corporate, sinful, Laodicean pride which has thwarted all of our Lord's attempts to bring healing, unity, and revival which would have made the finishing of our gospel task possible*. Either our Lord has delayed His coming and lied to us when He has said repeatedly that it is "near," or *we* have delayed it by our stubborn impenitence. Insisting on the former virtually destroys the Advent Movement; recognizing the latter alone can validate it. It is our corporate love of self that must be crucified, not the church, not its basic doctrines, not its prophet.

Our denominational history is in fact one continual call to repentance. At any moment, a righteous choice to repent will transform our view of our history into an appropriate *metanoia* as the practical effect of the "final atonement" or reconciliation with Christ. But sinful corporate or denominational pride will automatically nullify such a union with Him. We can find union with our Lord only in repentance.

"Just Like the Jews"

Our denominational parallel with the history of the ancient Jewish nation is striking. They were God's true denominated people, enjoying as much evidence of His favor as have we. Their pride in their denominational structure and organization was shown by their attitude towards the temple, which the Lord rebuked: "Trust ye not in lying words, saying, The temple of the Lord, The temple of the Lord, The temple of the Lord, are these" (Jeremiah 7:4). The "temple" to us is our modern worldwide organization. The Lord did indeed establish and bless the ancient temple, but the Jews' failure to accept denominational repentance is an illuminated warning to us:

> The same disobedience and failure which were seen in the Jewish church have characterized in a greater degree the people who have had this great light from Heaven in the last messages of warning. Shall we let the history of Israel be repeated in our experience? Shall we, like them, squander our opportunities and privileges until God shall permit oppression and persecution to come upon us? Will the work which might be performed in peace and comparative prosperity be left undone until it must be performed in days of darkness, under the pressure of trial and persecution?
>
> There is a terrible amount of guilt for which the church is responsible. (*Testimonies*, Vol. 5, pp. 456, 457.)

Whatever may be this "terrible amount of guilt for which the church is responsible," she is still the one object of the Lord's supreme regard. Without an understanding of the atonement of Christ, it is devastating to any individual's self-respect to come face to face with the full reality of his guilt. It is the same with the church body. In order to face this "terrible amount of guilt" without a devastating discouragement, the church also must understand that God's love for her as a body is unchanging, despite her guilt.

Numerous inspired statements liken our denominational failure to that of the Jews, most of which were written regarding the reaction against the message of the 1888 crisis in our history. A few examples follow:

> Since the time of the Minneapolis [1888] meeting, I have seen the state of the Laodicean church as never before. I have heard the rebuke of God spoken to those who feel so well satisfied, who know not their spiritual destitution. ... Like the Jews, many have closed their eyes lest they should see. (*Review and Herald*, August 26, 1890.)

> The Lord is at work, seeking to purify His people. ... But many have said by their indifferent attitude, "We want not Thy way, O God, but our own way ..."
>
> There is less excuse in our day for stubbornness and unbelief than there was for the Jews in the days of Christ. ... In our day greater light and greater evidence is given. ... Our sin and its retribution will be the greater, if we refuse to walk in the light. Many say, "If I had only lived in the days of Christ, I would not have wrested His words, or falsely

interpreted His instruction. I would not have rejected and crucified Him, as did the Jews;" but that will be proved by the way in which you deal with His message and His messengers today. The Lord is testing His people of today as He tested the Jews in their day. ... if with all the light that shone upon His ancient people, delineated before us, we travel over the same ground, cherish the same spirit, refuse to receive reproof and warning, then our guilt will be greatly augmented, and the condemnation that fell upon them will fall upon us, only it will be as much greater as our light is greater in this age than was their light in their age. (*Review and Herald*, April 11, 1893.)

All the universe of heaven witnessed the disgraceful treatment of Jesus Christ, represented by the Holy Spirit [at the 1888 Minneapolis session]. Had Christ been before them, they [the leaders] would have treated Him in a manner similar to that in which the Jews treated Christ. (*Special Testimonies*, Series A, No. 6, p. 20.)

In Minneapolis God gave precious gems of truth to His people in new settings. This light from heaven by some was rejected with all the stubbornness the Jews manifested in rejecting Christ. (*MS* 13, 1889.)

Men professing godliness have despised Christ in the person of His messengers. Like the Jews, they reject God's message. The Jews asked regarding Christ, Who is this? Is not this Joseph's son? He was not the Christ that the Jews had looked for. So today the agencies that God sends are not what men have looked for. (*Fundamentals of Christian Education*, p. 472.)

If the ministers will not receive the light, I want to give the people a chance; perhaps they may receive it. ... then you acknowledged that Sister White was right. But somehow it has changed now, and Sister White is different. Just like the Jewish nation. (*MS* 9, 1888: *Through Crisis to Victory*, p. 292.)

The question comes naturally, Why is the opposition to the 1888 message likened so often to the Jews' opposition to Christ? (There are actually scores of these statements.)

We have seen in our study of repentance that the bedrock sin of all mankind is hatred and rejection of Christ, manifested in His crucifixion. Repentance for this sin is where the miracle of the atonement takes place.

Our 1888 history illustrates this truth, and the inspired messenger of the Lord was quick to discern its significance. The 1888 Conference was a miniature Calvary. It afforded a public demonstration of the same spirit of unbelief and hatred of God's righteousness that inspired the Jews to murder the Son of God. This is obvious from the above statements.

The spirit that actuated the opposers of the message was not a minor misunderstanding, a temporary underestimate of the importance of a debated doctrine. *It was rebellion against God.*

How Our History Discloses Enmity Against God

Bear in mind that these facts in no way diminish the truth that the Seventh-day Adventist church was then and is now the "remnant church." The brethren who apposed the 1888 message were the true "angel of the church of the Laodiceans," and God had not cast them off, nor their "children" today. The simple fact is that they (that is "we," for we all participate together according to the principle of corporate identity) have something to repent about. Our denominational history makes Christ's call to repent come "alive." And the only reason it has not come "alive" sooner is that it has not been understood. The true history has been suppressed and denied.

Whereas the ancient Jews rejected their long-awaited Messiah, "we" rejected our long-awaited outpouring of the Holy Spirit in the "latter rain." The details are complementary:

(1) The Jews' Messiah was born in a stable, instead of in a palace; the beginning of the "latter rain" in 1888 was manifested in surprisingly humble circumstances.

(2) The Jews failed to discern in the anointed Jesus of Nazareth the Son of God in lowly guise; "we" failed to discern in the humble, young, and sometimes faulty messengers of 1888 the Lord's truly delegated messengers.

(3) The Jews feared that Jesus would destroy their denominational organization; "we" feared that the 1888 message would damage the character of the church and perhaps destroy its effectiveness through uplifting faith rather than the works of the law as the sole means of salvation.

(4) The callous, determined opposition of certain leaders of the Jews influenced many people to reject Jesus; the mysterious and persistent opposition of certain prominent leading brethren in the years that followed 1888 influenced many younger workers and the church at large either to disregard the message or to underestimate its importance.

(5) The Jewish nation never repented of their national sin and therefore never were able to recover the blessings that an acceptance of Jesus' lordship would have brought them; "we" have never as a denomination faced our corporate guilt and repented of "our" rejection of the beginning of the latter rain. For this reason we have never as yet enjoyed the full blessings of its outpouring. According to the following insight concerning the results of the 1888 unbelief, God's work could have been finished within a few years at that time:

> The influence that grew out of the resistance of light and truth at Minneapolis tended to make of no effect the light God had given to His people through the Testimonies. ...
>
> If every soldier of Christ had done his duty, if every watchman on the walls of Zion had given the trumpet a certain sound, the world might ere this have heard the message of warning. But the work is years behind. What account will be rendered to God for thus retarding the work? (Ellen G. White Letter, January 9, 1893, read February 28, 1893, to General Conference Session; 1893 *General Conference Bulletin*, p. 419.)

The evidence is remarkably emphatic and consistent. Ellen G. White did not waver from side to side in her analysis of what happened. There is no need to "explain" her statements. She is her own best interpreter.

To nurture pride and complacency by use of isolated extracts from her writings is a futile task. Equally hopeless is the attempt to wrest her statements toward a blanket condemnation of the church or its leadership. The obvious truth that commends itself to every candid student is that she believed to the end (1) that the Seventh-day Adventist church is the true "remnant church" of Bible prophecy, entrusted with the proclamation to the world of God's last gospel message of mercy; and (2) that repentance and humbling of heart before God is the only appropriate response that "we" can make that will enable Heaven to pour out the fullness of the Holy Spirit for the accomplishment of the task.

The Full Truth is Uplifting, Not Depressing

The temptation constantly intrudes to regard the full truth as somehow depressing or "negative." How much better to gloss over the facts and make ourselves feel good!

But the Lord says, "Ye shall know the truth, and the truth shall make you free." (John 8:32). Truth is always encouraging because truth is vitalized by love. Truth is divine. Therefore, the most encouraging and edifying news that can come to the church is the full knowledge of her alienated relationship to Jesus Christ as disclosed in His testimony and in the facts of her own history.

A simple fact becomes immediately relevant: a full and final reconciliation with the Lord that will lead to finishing His task on earth will accompany our experience of repentance.

It has been customary to speak of the 1888 message as a mere "re-emphasis" of the historic, Protestant doctrine of justification by faith as taught by the Reformers. This masks the truth of that era of our history as much as the Jews' way of speaking of a certain Rabbi from Galilee masks a purpose to deny His real identity. Just as Christ was indeed a Rabbi from Galilee, so the 1888 message was indeed justification and righteousness by faith. But just as Christ was far more than a Rabbi from Galilee, so the message was far more than a mere re-emphasis of the teaching of the Reformers of old.

> Luther had a great work to do in reflecting to others the light which God had permitted to shine upon him; yet he did not receive all the light which was to be given to the world. From that time to this, new light has been continually shining upon the Scriptures, and new truths have been constantly unfolding. (*The Great Controversy*, pp. 148, 149.)

That "light" will continue to unfold until it lightens the earth with glory under the ministration of the long-awaited "latter rain" and "loud cry;" the 1888 message was the beginning of its final manifestation. Our great world task is as yet unfinished largely because of a failure to relate ourselves aright to that divine manifestation of truth. (See *Selected Messages*, Book 1, pp. 234, 235.)

We Are No More Righteous Than Our "Fathers"

We today may feel distressed that any of our brethren of a past generation should have reacted against what the Lord intended to be the beginning of the finishing of His work. We may even feel thankful that we have not been tested as they were. "We were not alive then and therefore cannot be guilty as they were. They were individually responsible to God; they are in their graves; we are innocent, fortunately removed from their temptation by nearly a century."

But the Bible principle of corporate guilt sheds an entirely different light on the matter. We may confess not only what we superficially see as our own iniquity, but also the iniquity of our fathers "with their trespass which they have trespassed" against the Lord. (Leviticus 26:40-42). We know that it is not unfair of the Lord to withhold from us further showers of the latter rain, for until we understand and repent in the same way that the Lord required ancient Israel to understand and repent of their past history, it can be said of us in truth, "Great is the wrath of the Lord that is kindled against us, because our fathers have not hearkened unto the words of this book, to do according unto all which is written concerning us" (2 Kings 22:13). Surely we can pray as did Ezra, "O my God, I am ashamed and blush to lift up my face to Thee, my God: for *our* iniquities are increased over our heads, and our trespass is grown up unto the heavens. Since the days of our fathers have we been in a great trespass unto this, day" (Ezra 9:6, 7).

Daniel's Corporate Repentance

Our position before the Lord closely parallels that of Israel in the days of Daniel. Here the principle of corporate guilt and corporate repentance comes into sharp focus.

Daniel could have argued before the Lord, "Some of us and some of our fathers were true, Lord; look how faithful Shadrach, Meshach, Abednego, and I have been! *We* have practiced health reform, *we* have received all the light You gave us! Remember how some of our 'fathers' in Jerusalem, as Jeremiah for example, Baruch, and a few others, stood nobly for the truth in times of apostasy. We are not *all* guilty, Lord!"

But what did Daniel pray? Notice his use of the corporate "we":

O Lord, righteousness belongeth unto Thee, but unto *us* confusion faces, as at this day; to the men of Judah, and to the inhabitants of Jerusalem, and unto *all Israel*, that are near, and that are far off. ... O Lord, to *us* belongeth confusion of face, to our kings, to our princes, and to our fathers, because *we* have sinned against Thee. ... Yea, *all Israel* have transgressed Thy law, even by departing, that they might not obey Thy voice; therefore, the curse is poured upon us, and the oath that is written in the law of Moses the servant of God, because *we* have sinned against Him.

... For *our* sins, and for the iniquities of *our* fathers, Jerusalem and Thy people are become a reproach to all that are about us. ... I was speaking and praying and confessing my sin *and* the sin of my people Israel. (Daniel 9:7-20.)

The result of this humble, honest recognition of corporate guilt is well-known. What will be the result of a similar recognition of our own measure of corporate guilt? How could it be anything other than the restoration of the "latter rain" and the "loud cry"?

As we have seen in previous chapters, the principle of individual and corporate guilt and repentance centers in the cross of Calvary. "The spirit of grace and of supplications" is poured on "the house of David and the inhabitants of Jerusalem" when God's people "look upon Him whom they have pierced" (Zechariah 12:10). The fact that we were not physically, personally present at Calvary is seen to make no difference.

The fact that we were not personally present in 1888 likewise will be seen to make no difference. The sin of our "fathers" is "our" sin. Christ Himself, in His own flesh, has shown us the way to experience a repentance for sins of which we have not thought ourselves individually and personally responsible. If He, the sinless One, repented in behalf of the sins of the whole world, surely we can repent in behalf of the sins of our "fathers," whose denominational "children" we are today!

Did the 1901 Conference Cancel the 1888 Unbelief?

Sincere members of the remnant church have assumed that the 1901 General Conference was the scene for an "about-face" and reformation that undid the rejection of the 1888 message and cancelled out its sad consequences. This view requires the parallel assumption that the "latter rain" and the "loud cry" have been progressing since the 1901 Session. This is the historical basis of the popular "all is well" school of thought.

It is true that the 1901 Session did result in great blessings to the world-wide organization of the church. But it is also clear that the results of that meeting in no way show that a deep spiritual reformation occurred that reversed the rejecting of the beginning of the "latter rain." Ellen G. White wrote to a friend a few months after the 1901 Session:

> The result of the last General Conference [1901] has been the greatest, the most terrible sorrow of my life. No change was made. The spirit that should have been brought into the whole work as the result of the meeting, was not brought in because men did not receive the testimonies of the Spirit of God. As they went to their several fields of labor, they did not walk in the light that the Lord had flashed upon their pathway, but carried into their work the wrong principles that had been prevailing in the work at Battle Creek. (Letter to Judge Jesse Arthur, Elmshaven, January 14, 1903.)

As the result of this impenitence, the finishing of the work was delayed an indefinite time. The following quotation is well known:

> We may have to remain here in this world because of insubordination many more years, as did the children of Israel, but for Christ's sake His people should not add sin to sin by charging God with the consequence of their own wrong course of action. (Letter December 7, 1901; M-184, 1901.)

Even so, it was not too late then to engage in an experience of repentance. Mrs. White did not use the phrase "denominational repentance," but she expressed the principle. "All" needed to participate:

> But if all now would only see and confess and repent of their own course of action in departing from the truth of God, and following human devising, then the Lord would pardon. (*Idem.*)

In sober moments we realize that revival and reformation are needed in every aspect of our vast world-wide work. Every department of our organization needs the infilling of the Holy Spirit—educational, medical, evangelistic, pastoral, financial, institutional, publishing, Administrative. No end of books could be written detailing all the minutiae of our needs. We can spend decades to come in wringing our hands about them.

Much the same situation existed in the days of John the Baptist. He could have spent several lifetimes trying to encompass all the needs for repentance in his day. He preferred to lay "the axe … unto the root of the trees" (Matthew 3:10).

To repent of "our" rejection of the "beginning " of the latter Rain is to lay the axe "unto the root" of our present problem.

There remains in our search for repentance one more question: What will be the practical results of corporate and denominational repentance?

CHAPTER 10

REPENTANCE: PATH TO CHRISTLIKE LOVE

If "God is love," love is power. The final manifestation of the Holy Spirit will be simply a demonstration by the church of the love of God:

> It is the darkness of misapprehension of God that is enshrouding the world. Men are losing their knowledge of His character. It has been misunderstood and misinterpreted. At this time a message from God is to be proclaimed, a message illuminating in its influence and saving in its power. His character is to be made known. Into the darkness of the world is to be shed the light of His glory, the light of His goodness, mercy, and truth.
>
> This is a work outlined by the prophet Isaiah in the words, "Oh Jerusalem, that bringeth good tidings, lift up thy voice with strength."
>
> Those who wait for the bridegroom's coming are to say to the people, "Behold you God." The last rays of merciful light, the last message of mercy to be given to the world, is a revelation of His character of love. The children of God are to manifest His glory. In their own life and character they are to reveal what the grace of God has done for them. (*Christ's Object Lessons*, pp. 415, 416.)

Jesus included the finishing of His work when He said, "By this shall all men know that you are my disciples, if ye have love one to another" (John 13:35).

For over a hundred years we have sensed the need for that love.* Local churches all over the world long to be able to reveal it, but feel hampered by inadequacy and contradictory influences that work to negate it. Obviously Satan hates the idea of such love really succeeding. Due to his "making war" against the "remnant church" from within as well as from without, after all these years we still are forced to recognize that this ultimate manifestation of love is yet future. No one can successfully point to a time in our past history and say, "Here the latter rain was received, and here these final prophecies were fulfilled."

---

* See *Testimonies*, Vol. 3, p. 187; Vol. 6, p. 398; *Acts of the Apostles*, p. 580.

Love, the Fire in the Coal

When that love does impregnate the church as fire permeates the coal, she will become super-efficient in soul winning. Each congregation, "Jerusalem" to its local community, will be what Christ would be to that community were He there in the flesh. He inspired with hope "the roughest and most unpromising," encouraged those who were "discouraged, sick, tempted, fallen," saved those "who were fighting a hand-to-hand battle with the adversary of souls." So will the church become a duplicate of Christ's power to redeem lost people.

This will not be done by bright advertising schemes or promotion methods. The Holy Spirit will do something for the *heart* because the church members will receive the "mind of Christ." "Miracles will be wrought, the sick will be healed, and signs and wonders will follow the believers. ... The rays of light penetrate everywhere, the truth is seen in its clearness, and the honest children of God sever the bands which have held them. ... A large number take their stand upon the Lord's side!' (*The Great Controversy*, p. 612).

What could those "rays of light" be except a clear example of the love of God seen in His people? One's mind staggers to try to imagine the joy that will flow like a river when the word of the Lord goes forth in glory and power and human hearts meet Christ and find in Him their soul's longing!

When one prays for the Lord to use him to win a soul, he can never know who that person may turn out to be. We may have hoped He would use us to win some "good" person; we may discover that He wants us to win someone we think of as "bad." We think of our congregation as a comfortable, exclusive religious club when the Lord declares that it is "an house of prayer for *all* people," including "sinners" we haven't thought much about.

It is pathetic to try to limit love to "good" people. Any love so restricted ceases to be love. It stands revealed for what it is—naked selfishness. Real love is not dependent on the beauty or the goodness of an object, as is our natural human affection. We "like" somebody who is nice. But it is impossible for us to love somebody who is not nice, unless an entirely different kind of love takes over the control of our hearts. That kind of love is what the New Testament calls "agape."

Here is an example of what it is: "God commendeth His love (*agape*) toward us in that while we were yet *sinners*, Christ died for us.... When we were *enemies*, we were reconciled to God by the death of His Son" (Romans 5:8, 10). "I say unto you, love [the same word] your enemies, bless them that curse you, do good to them that hate you, and pray for them which despitefully use you" (Matthew 5:44). We are to make the "sun" of our love "to rise on the evil and on the good," to show our mercy and compassion both on "the just and on the unjust" (verses 45-48).

Why does God waste His gifts on "bad" people? Why send sunlight and rain on "enemies"? The answer is that God has something that is not natural for us to have—agape. If we could manipulate the bounties of nature, we would make a difference. And we would probably feel that our method of discriminating between "good" and "bad" people would be more efficient in persuading the "bad" to become "good" than God's way of showering blessings on both alike without any sign that He likes one type of person better than the other.

But our Father in heaven is "perfect" in His love for the unworthy. When we learn such love, He will call us "perfect," too, His true "children."

Such love filling the church will accomplish wonders we now hardly dream of. We have no idea how many people are counted by the Lord as His, scattered all around us far and near, whom now we consider hopeless. Yet they are just as much His as was Mary Magdalene, or the thief on the cross. The moment we try to be selective in our "love" and feel, "I want to invite this person to come to Christ because he is nice, but I don't care to win that person," we forfeit connection with the Holy Spirit.

As the "Pharisees and scribes murmured," we are too easily scandalized because "this Man receiveth sinners" (Luke 15:1, 2). But the greater the evil of the sinner, the greater is God's glory in changing him:

> The divine Teacher bears with the erring through all their perversity. His love does not grow cold; His efforts to win them do not cease. With outstretched arms He waits to welcome again and again the erring, the rebellious, and even the apostate.... Though all are precious in His sight, the rough, sullen, stubborn dispositions draw most heavily upon His sympathy and love; for He traces from cause

to effect. The one who is most easily tempted, and is most inclined to err, is the special object of His solicitude. (*Education*, p. 294.)

Repentance Lights the Fire in the Coal

Now, to be practical, how can we learn this kind of love?

There is no way except by seeing Christ as He is. He is very different from what many confused ideas have supposed He is. Perfectly sinless, nevertheless He experienced a corporate repentance "in behalf of the sins of the world." He knew how weak He was apart from strength from His Father. He knew He could fall. Born in the river that sweeps us into sin through the force of its undertow, He stood firm on the rock of faith in His Father, even when it appeared that He was forsaken. The Father sent His Son "in the likeness of sinful flesh." In very truth He is our "brother." He bore the guilt of "every sinner." No one's heart was locked for which He did not therefore have the key.

Zechariah says that the greatest event ever to happen to the church in the last days will be this new vision of Christ: "They shall look upon Me whom they have pierced, and they shall mourn for Him." Here is a clear picture. When we realize that we are the ones who have crucified Him, and when we "look upon Him" with understanding, we shall realize a new sense of oneness with Him and sympathy for Him. We will feel toward Him as a parent feels toward an only son, a great warmth of affection that will cancel out the appeal of all worldly allurement. This experience will indeed be a miracle.

The point of Zechariah's prophecy is that corporate repentance felt for corporate guilt will trigger this marvelous experience. Then will come the free-flowing love for sinners we long to achieve. The point is that this ability to feel for and to love every sinner was not a supernatural endowment imparted to Christ exclusively because He was the Son of God; *it was the direct result of His experience of corporate repentance.*

We may not in our human judgment be guilty of the sin of another, but once we get the idea that we too are born with a carnal mind which is "enmity against God," we sense how in truth that sin is as natural to us as it has been to another, and how it would have been acted out in us if it had not been for the grace of Christ and for the lack of equal circumstances or opportunity. He who has the "mind of Christ" will have the repentance of Christ. The closer He comes to Christ, the more he will identify himself with every sinner on earth. Christ asks "the angel of the church of the Laodiceans" to repent no more than He Himself has repented. It is treason to Him to repent less!

Righteousness by Faith and Repentance

Only a repentance such as this can make sense of the expression, "The Lord our Righteousness." The one who knows that Christ is *all* his righteousness will know that he is himself *all* sin. The one who feels that by nature he has at least some righteousness of his own will feel he is that much better than the sinner. Feeling so, he will know nothing of Christ. Christ to him will be a stranger. And so will the sinner be a stranger to him. When Wesley saw a drunkard lying in the gutter, he said, "There, but for the grace of Christ, am I." Evidently he must have felt it deep inside, for if the remark had been a mere cliche to him, he would never have been able to change as many lives as he did.

Self-righteous "saints" abhor the truth of Christ's righteousness. They resent the contrition that is implicit in seeing in Christ *all* their righteousness. They shrink with abhorrence from putting themselves in the place of the sinner, the alcoholic, the dope addict, the criminal, the prostitute, the rebel, the mentally ill. They say in heart, "I could never sink to such a depth!"

So long as they feel thus, they are powerless to speak as Jesus did the effective word to help such. Their love for souls is frozen by their impenitence. Restrained and restricted, it ceases to be love. They decline to enter the kingdom of heaven themselves through letting the Holy Spirit melt down their deep-frozen hearts, and they actually "shut up the kingdom of heaven against men," barring the way so that neither "Mary Magdalene" nor "the thief on the cross" can find a path to get in. Blessed would be the millstone to be hung around the necks of such people, and blessed would be their drowning in the sea, said Jesus, rather than that they should face in the Judgment the results of their hard lifelong lovelessness. "It were better not to live than to exist day by day devoid of that love which Christ has enjoined upon His children" (*Counsels to Teachers*, p. 266).

It is this impenitence that is directly hindering the coming of the "latter rain" for the effective finishing of the gospel work on earth. According to Christ's call to "the angel of the church of the Laodiceans," it is time now for us to understand that the guilt of the whole world's sin is ours, "mine," apart from the grace of Christ. I am the whole world's sin, its frustrated enmity against God, its despair, its rebellion—all is mine; and if Christ were to withdraw from me His grace, I would embody the whole of its evil, for "in me, that is in my flesh, dwelleth no good thing."

This is the reason why the repentance Christ begs us to accept takes us back to Calvary. It is impossible to repent truly of minor sin without repenting of the major sin which underlies all other sin. Without seeing that truth, repentance is an empty word. True repentance is nothing short of an "after-perception" of our guilt shown "in behalf of the human race" in crucifying Christ.

There is a close relation between righteousness by faith and corporate identity. As we have seen, the underlying idea behind the "message of Christ's righteousness" is that I possess not a shred of righteousness of my own. If I have none of my own, what do I have which is rightfully my own?

The answer is *sin*.

But how much sin do I have? Only a little? No, I am *all* sin. It follows that the New Testament idea of "righteousness by faith" is built on the principle of corporate guilt and corporate repentance. By perfect corporate repentance, the sinner accepts the gift of contrition for all sin of which he is potentially capable, and not merely for the few sins which he thinks he has actually committed himself. Thus in turn he receives the gift from Christ of potential righteousness equal to His own perfection, at present far beyond the sinner's capacity. But it is just as real as the sense of potential guilt he has realized in behalf of the sins of the whole world.

The Miracle-working Power of Repentance

If the sinner narrows his repentance within the limits of those few "little" sins he feels personally guilty of actually committing, he likewise narrows his reception of righteousness from Christ to equally restricted limits of his poor idea of what it should be. The result: pride, complacency, pathetic ignorance, and lukewarmness. Such an impenitent "saint" is living as far below his capacity for life as a sea gull made to fly the ocean who bathes in a birdbath.

Miracles will become natural to the one willing to receive the gift of corporate repentance from Christ. Such love for sinners "hopeth all things." Like the Lord Himself, the repentant sinner "delighteth in mercy" and discovers his greatest pleasure to be taking apparently hopeless material and making these people subjects of God's grace. Think of the beautiful work you will be able to do once you receive in "the mind of Christ" His own experience of repentance:

> Tell the poor desponding ones who have gone astray that they need not despair. Though they have erred, and have not been building a right character, God has joy to restore to them, even the joy of His salvation. He delights to take apparently hopeless material, those through whom Satan has worked, and make them the subjects of His grace. ... Tell them there is healing, cleansing for every soul. There is a place for them at the Lord's table. (*Christ's Object Lessons*, p. 234.)

Such delight in transforming "apparently hopeless material" is "the joy of the Lord." The church is invited to enter into it, now.

We have reached the time in history when individual repentance need no longer be confused with corporate repentance. Paul's doctrine must now come into its own, and the seed sown nearly two thousand years ago begin to bear the blessed fruit that the whole creation has groaned and travailed together in pain to see.

The kind of repentance Christ calls for in the Laodicean message is already a concept beginning to be realized. When one member in a congregation falls into sin, a little reflection can convince many of the members that they actually share in the guilt. Had we been more watchful, more alert, more kind-hearted, more ready to speak "a word in season to him that is weary," more effective in proclaiming the pure truth of the gospel, we might have saved the erring member from his fall. With knowledgeable pastoral care, almost any church can at present be led to feel this corporate concern.

It is encouraging therefore to trust that within this generation the same sense of loving concern can be realized on a worldwide scale. When this time comes (and it will come unless hindered and opposed), there will be a heart-unity and corporate concern between races and nationalities seldom seen as yet. The fulfillment of Christ's ideal will be seen on all levels and among all groups. The winter of frozen inhibitions and fears will give way to a glorious spring and summer where the loves and sympathies that God has implanted in our souls will find true and pure expression to one another. Racial and cultural barriers will come down. It will be impossible any longer to feel superior to or patronizing toward people whose race, nationality, or cultural milieu was deprived. With the "mind of Christ," you automatically feel yourself on their level, and a bond of sympathy and fellowship is established "in Him." Again, this will be a miracle, but one that will follow the laws of grace.

This repentance will take us a step further in the path to spiritual maturity. Instead of limiting itself to a shared repentance in behalf of our contemporary generation of the living, it will take in past generations as well. Paul's idea, "As the body is one, and hath many members, ... so also is Christ," will be seen to include the "body" of Christ in all time.

Already we can sense the concern "in Christ" which the Holy Spirit imparts to the church, so that we can share the guilt of a fellow-sinner who is our contemporary; it is only another step to share the guilt of one who is not contemporary. Thus a repentance becomes possible for the sins of previous generations, and Moses' command is found possible of obedience (Leviticus 26:40). Thus the "final atonement" becomes a reality, and the pre-Advent judgment concluded.

The perfect "one body" experience will fill the church. While it is true that there will be a "shaking," and some, perhaps many, will be shaken out, the inspired word that describes this process of separation clearly implies that a true remnant of believers in Christ will remain. The "shaking" of the tree or branches will certainly mean that "gleaning grapes shall be left in it" (cf. Isaiah 17:6; 24:13). Those who are "shall lift up their voice, they shall sing for the majesty of the Lord" (verse 14). Those who are shaken out will only make "manifest that they were not all of us" (1 John 2:19). God's work will go forward unhindered, but rather greatly strengthened.

In this time, the church will be united and coordinated like a healthy human body. Church trials will be a thing of the past. Backbiting, evil-surmising, gossip, even forgetfulness of the needs of others, will be overcome. The listening ear having learned to be sensitive to the call of the Holy Spirit, the conviction of duty will be heard and acted upon. When He says to one as He said to Philip the deacon, "Go near, and join thyself to this chariot," the obedient response will be immediate; and a soul will be won as Philip won the Ethiopian official from Candace's royal court. At last the Holy Spirit will find a perfectly responsive "temple" in which to dwell; and rejoicing over His people with singing, the Lord will gladly bring into their fellowship all His "people" now scattered in Babylon.

Miracles of heart-healing will come precisely as if Christ Himself were present in the flesh to minister them. Chasms of estrangement will be bridged over. Marital dissensions will find solutions that have evaded the best efforts of counselors and psychiatrists. Broken homes will be cemented together in the bonds of such divine love that elicits ultimate contrition and repentance from believing hearts. Harps now silent will ring with melody when the strings are touched by this hand of love. Bewildered and frustrated youth will see a revelation of Christ never before discerned. Satan's enchantment of drugs, liquor, immorality, and rebellion will lose its hold, and the pure, joyous tide of youthful devotion to Christ will flow as never before to the praise of His grace.

The watching world and the vast universe beyond will behold with joy the final demonstration of the fruits of Christ's sacrifice. In a profound sense hardly dreamed of by the pioneers of the Advent Movement, the heavenly sanctuary, nerve center of God's great controversy with Satan, will be "cleansed," justified, set before the universe in its right light.

The Church a Powerhouse of Ministering Love

Such an experience of repentance will transform the church into a dynamo of love. The strongholds of Satan will be pulled down before it. No church will have seating capacity for the converted sinners who will stream into it. Because He took the steps the sinner must take in repentance, Christ was enabled to pass by no human being as "worthless;" He broke the spell of the world's enchantment for the wealthy, the pleasure loving, the vain; He inspired with hope the "roughest and most unpromising;" He cast out "devils." Corporate and denominational repentance is the "whole church" experiencing this same Christlike love and empathy for all for whom He died.

Those who say, "It's too good to be true! It just can't happen! I'll never see it!" should be careful how they react to the heavenly vision of success. In the days of Elisha, Samaria suffered a terrible siege famine. "A donkey's head cost eighty pieces of silver, and half a pound of dove's dung cost five pieces of silver." Acts of frightful cannibalism were well known. Blaming the Lord for it all, the king wanted to kill the prophet. (Are the present attacks on Ellen White also the result of a similar motivation?)

Elisha responded by promising that within twenty-four hours "ten pounds of the best wheat or twenty pounds of barley" would be selling in the city gates for only "one piece of silver." The instant reaction of "the personal attendant of the king" was that such plenty would be too good to be true. "'That can't happen,' he responded,"—not even if the Lord himself were to send grain at once!"

"You will see it happen, but you won't get any of the food," Elisha replied. The Bible story continues, "It so happened that the king of Israel had put the city gate under the command of the officer who was his personal attendant." When the Lord suddenly frightened the invading Syrians and they left their huge supplies for the starving Israelites, the officer was "trampled to death by the people at the city gate." (See 2 Kings 7:1-20, GNB).

Our unbelief in this "time of the latter rain" will likewise shut us out from taking part in the glorious experience that the Lord foretells for His people once they repent in obedience to His command. Numerous inspired statements confirm the vision of the "whole church" within history fully experiencing such blessing.

An example is the following vision of a repentance yet future, but which is to be experienced by the leadership of the church. Note that it will be a repentance so deep and effective that previously unknown and unrealized sin will be brought to consciousness. Note also the reference to the prophecy of Zechariah 12:10 of God's people sensing their involvement in the sin of piercing Christ:

> In the night season I was in my dreams in a large meeting, with ministers, their wives, and their children. I wondered that the company present was mostly made up of ministers and their families. The prophecy of Malachi was brought before them in connection with Daniel, Zephaniah, Haggai, and Zechariah. The teaching of these books was carefully investigated. The building of the temple, and the temple service, were considered. There was close searching of the Scriptures in regard to the sacred character of all that appertained to the temple service. Through the prophets, God has given a delineation of what will come to pass in the last days of this earth's history; and the Jewish economy is full of instruction for us.
>
> The offering of beasts ... the rivers of blood ... provision for the poor to receive the comforts of life ... the whole sanctuary service ... All these things were closely studied by the company before me in

my dream. Scripture was compared with scripture, and application was made of the word of God to our own time. After a diligent searching of the Scriptures, there was a period of silence. A very solemn impression was made upon the people. The deep moving of the Spirit of God was manifest among us. All were troubled, all seemed to be convicted, burdened, and distressed, and they saw their own life and character represented in the word of God, and the Holy Spirit was making the application to their hearts.

Conscience was aroused. The record of past days was making its disclosure of the vanity of human inventions. The Holy Spirit brought all things to their remembrance. As they reviewed their past history, there were revealed defects of character that ought to have been discerned and corrected. They saw how through the grace of Christ the character should have been transformed. The workers had known the sorrow of defeat in the work intrusted to their hands, when they should have had victory.

The Holy Spirit presented before them Him whom they had offended. They saw that God will not only reveal himself as a God of mercy and forgiveness and long forbearance, but by terrible things in righteousness He will make it manifest that He is not a man that He should lie.

Words were spoken by One, saying, "The hidden, inner life will be revealed. As if reflected in a mirror, all the inward working of the character will be made manifest. The Lord would have you examine your own lives, and see how vain is human glory." "Deep calleth unto deep at the noise of thy waterspouts; all thy waves and thy billows are gone over me. Yet the Lord will command His loving-kindness in the daytime, and in the night His song shall be with me, and my prayer unto the God of my life." (*Review and Herald*, February 4, 1902.)

If it were in your power to "vote" that this experience take place now, would you want it to?

Well, the vote *is* in your power, and mine.

And we will exercise it, one way or the other.

www.ingramcontent.com/pod-product-compliance
Lightning Source LLC
Chambersburg PA
CBHW060407080526
44583CB00012B/497